12-6-21

FAST FRENCH

By the same author

French in 32 Lessons
German in 32 Lessons
Spanish in 32 Lessons
Italian in 32 Lessons

and, for the more advanced student

Français Parlé
Gesprochenes Deutsch
Español Hablado
Italiano Parlato

The Gimmick Series

FAST FRENCH

Adrienne

W · W · NORTON & COMPANY
New York · London

Library of Congress Cataloging in Publication Data
Adrienne.
  Fast French.
    1. French language—Grammar—1950–   2. French
language—Text-books for foreign speakers—English.
I. Title.
PC2112.A28   1984   448.3′421   84–6106

ISBN 0-393-31669-6

W. W. Norton & Company, Inc., 500 Fifth Avenue, New York, NY 10110
W. W. Norton & Company Ltd., 10 Coptic Street, London WC1A 1PU

2 3 4 5 6 7 8 9 0

'I went through the woods for a
walk in the rain . . . and as I
walked my soul was freed from
pain.'

                    Jean Seberg

'Je m'asseyais le dos contre l'écorce
d'un redwood et puis j'essayais de lui
prendre quelque chose, de lui voler
quelque chose, en douce, mine de rien,
par contact subreptice, lui soutirer deux
sous de dureté, d'impassibilité, d'indif-
férence, de je vous emmerde tous. Ça
ne marchait jamais.

                    Romain Gary
                    La Nuit Sera Calme

I'm very grateful to Sabine Bossan and
Elisabeth de Lesparda for their collaboration

Preface

What is fast French?

The man or woman doing business in France, the tourist, the student at school, all have one basic need: to express themselves so that they can be understood — and understand — at the simplest level. Specialized vocabulary, and the nuances of grammar can come next in my more advanced books. Here I present the basic grammar, and the 1300 most useful words and expressions. *Fast French* is an indispensable auxiliary text for students of French because it incorporates structured teaching of vocabulary, and a language is, above all, words.

To have mastered this book means that you will never be tongue-tied. You will always be able to say something to get your meaning over.

How to use this book

1) Each of the 24 lessons has:
   a) a grammatical 'structure' that you need to understand thoroughly
   b) a page of vocabulary at the end of it, which is carefully laid out to make it easy for you to learn it by heart
   c) a series of exercises to which you should write out the answers — this helps to impress them on your memory — before you check with the key at the end of the book to see if you have got them right

2) Begin by reading the 'structure', which has been enclosed in a 'box', so that you can grasp the essence of it at once. Make absolutely sure you understand it.

3) Then go through the page of vocabulary at the end of the lesson. Learn it by heart (and get someone to test you, if you can!).

4) Now you are ready to tackle the exercises. Remember that they must be written out the first time you do them.

5) Finally, see how you did, by looking at the key at the back of the book.

French isn't an easy language for English-speakers to learn. The grammar is more complicated than English, which is the simplest in the world to learn! So, remember to be patient. Work systematically, a little *every day*, and learning all the words *by heart!* Mastering the grammar is no use if you have nothing to say, no words to use! So, jump in, and

BONNE CHANCE!

A special note for parents

If you are using this book to help your child learn French (and perhaps brushing up your own), remember that one does not learn a language by osmosis. Systematic study is essential, so be sure that the exercises are written out for each lesson, and be sure to test each other on the vocabulary words. This is the best way to make sure that what you have learnt stays with you.

A special note for teachers

This book has 24 well-filled lessons. A class should be able to study one a week. Checking that new vocabulary words have been well-learnt is essential. You should therefore give short written tests each week, with lists of words or sentences from the lesson to translate.

Table des Matières/Contents

en train de + infinitive = -ing, in the
midst of
être sur le point de = to be about to
avoir envie de . . . = to feel like

Leçon 1/Lesson 1

ÊTRE = TO BE

je **suis**	= I am
tu **es**/vous **êtes**	= you are
il **est**	= he is
elle **est**	= she is
c'**est**	= it is
nous **sommes**	= we are
vous **êtes**	= you are
ils/elles **sont**	= they are

Est-ce que tu es/vous êtes anglais? = Are you English?
Oui, je suis anglais. = Yes, I'm English.

careful! — generally, for the feminine of adjectives, add an 'e' (anglais →
anglais**e**)
— generally, for the plural of adjectives, add an 's' (triste → triste**s**)
— 'vous' is more formal: use it for both singular and plural; 'tu' is
used for friends, family, etc

translate:

a   1) Est-ce que vous êtes français? — Oui, je suis français.
2) Est-ce que tu es triste? — Oui, je suis triste.
3) Est-ce que vous êtes désolés? — Oui, nous sommes désolés.
4) Est-ce que tu es grand? — Oui, je suis grand.

b   1) Are you happy? — Yes, I'm happy.
2) Are you tired? — Yes, I'm tired.
3) Are you short? — Yes, I'm short.
4) Are you young? — Yes, I'm young.

NOTE the sign ≠ means 'opposite associated'; see page 9, etc.

1

Est-ce qu'il est heureux? = Is he happy?
Oui, il est heureux. = Yes, he's happy.

Est-ce qu'ils sont médecins? = Are they doctors?
Oui, ils sont médecins. = Yes, they're doctors.

careful! — generally, for the plural of nouns, add an 's' (médecin →
médecins)

Est-ce que c'est joli? = Is it pretty?
Oui, c'est joli. = Yes, it's pretty.

translate:

a 1) Excusez-moi, je suis désolé.
   2) Il est heureux.
   3) Ils sont vieux.
   4) Nous sommes jeunes.
   5) Est-ce que c'est bleu?
   6) Encore? Oui, encore une fois.
   7) Je suis grande.
   8) Vous êtes américaine.

b 1) How are you?
   2) It's ugly.
   3) Is she French?
   4) They're sorry.
   5) She's short.
   6) We're happy.
   7) See you soon.
   8) Good morning!

VOCABULAIRE/VOCABULARY

	translation	synonym/ associated	opposite/ associated
1) Français, français	(the) French (people), French (language)	anglais = English, américain = American	
2) tôt	early	à l'heure = on time	tard = late
3) Comment allez-vous?	How are you?		bien merci = fine, thank you
4) Bonjour	Good morning, Good afternoon		Bonsoir = Good evening, Bonne nuit = Good night
5) fatigué	tired	qui a sommeil = sleepy, épuisé = exhausted	
6) Je suis désolé	I'm sorry	Excusez-moi! = Excuse me!	
7) heureux	happy		triste = sad, malheureux = unhappy
8) joli	pretty		laid = ugly
9) jeune	young		vieux = old
10) grand	tall		petit = short
11) bleu, rouge	blue, red	bleu marine = navy blue, vert = green	
12) oui	yes		non = no
13) Salut!	Hallo!, Hi!	À bientôt! = See you soon!	Au revoir = Goodbye, Salut! = Bye!
14) encore	again	encore une fois = once more	

Leçon 2/Lesson 2

je ne suis pas	= I'm not
tu n'es pas/vous n'êtes pas	= you aren't
il ⎫	he ⎫
elle ⎬ **n'est pas**	= she ⎬ isn't
ce ⎭	it ⎭
nous ne sommes pas	= we aren't
vous n'êtes pas	= you aren't
ils/elles ne sont pas	= they aren't

careful! — the French present is also used to translate our present perfect: il est médecin depuis deux ans = he's been a doctor for two years

Est-ce que tu es/vous êtes espagnol?	= Are you Spanish?
Non, je ne suis pas espagnol.	= No, I am not Spanish.

careful! — 'Êtes-vous espagnol?' is a less usual way of asking the question.

Est-ce que c'est intéressant?	= Is it interesting?
Non, ce n'est pas intéressant.	= No, it isn't interesting.

translate:

a
1) Qu'est-ce qui ne va pas? *Whats wrong   whats not going on*
2) Il n'est pas bête. *he is not stupid*
3) Ce n'est pas chaud. *it is not hot*
4) Ils ne sont pas docteurs. *They are not Drs &*
5) Ils ne sont pas faibles. *They are not weak*
6) Est-ce que tu comprends? *Do you understand?*
7) Ce n'est pas long. *it is not long*
8) Nous ne sommes pas infirmières. *We are not nurses*

b
1) I'm not foolish. *Ju ne suis pas bete.*
2) It isn't great. *se ne pas grand*
3) You aren't stupid. *tu ne pas bete*
4) It isn't early. *est nu est pas tôt*
5) What's the matter?
6) He isn't nice. *il nes pas)*
7) He isn't strong. *il ne est pas fort*
8) Thank you! You're welcome! *merci / pas de qua   de rien*

loin (lew-an) far

CONTRAIRES/OPPOSITES 1

1) **Tom est gros**
(Tom's fat)
≠ **mince**
(thin)

2) **Je suis riche**
(I'm rich)
≠ **pauvre**
(poor)

3) **Jane est forte**
(Jane's strong)
≠ **faible**
(weak)

4) **C'est grand**
(It's big)
≠ **petit**
(small)

5) **Je suis jeune** ~~vielle~~ *fem*
(I'm young)
≠ **vieux** – *vielle*
(old) *fem.*

6) **Elle est jolie/belle**
(She's pretty/beautiful)
≠ **laide** *lecb)* *led*
(ugly) *fem* *mas.*

7) **Vous êtes sale**
(You're dirty)
≠ **propre**
(clean)

8) **Je suis ici**
(I'm here)
≠ **là**
(there)

9) **Le livre est facile/simple** *Sample*
(The book's easy/simple)
≠ **difficile/dur**
(difficult/hard)

10) **La film est intéressant/passionnant**
(The film's interesting/exciting)
≠ **ennuyeux** *on we you – mas*
(boring/dull) *on we youre –*
fem

translate:

a 1) Elle est pauvre et je suis pauvre aussi.
   2) Il est ennuyeux et tu es ennuyeux aussi.
   3) Il est laid mais il est gentil.
   4) Nous sommes petits et minces.
   5) Les livres ne sont pas chers et ils sont neufs.
   6) Vous êtes vieux et sale aussi.
   7) Je suis jeune et belle.
   8) Le livre n'est pas bon marché, mais il est beau.

b 1) I'm rich and she's rich also.
   2) We're strong and intelligent too.
   3) You aren't dirty, but he's dirty.
   4) She's pretty and you are pretty too.
   5) He's tall and thin.
   6) The lesson isn't easy, but it's interesting.
   7) The nurse's here and the doctor is too.
   8) They aren't expensive, but they're beautiful.

VOCABULAIRE/VOCABULARY

	translation	synonym/ associated	opposite/ associated
1) aussi	also, too	et = and	non plus = not either *plu*
2) très	very	tout à fait = quite	un peu = a little
3) mais	but	de = of, ou = or	
4) nouveau	new	neuf	vieux = old
5) (le) médecin *med san)*	doctor	(le) docteur	(l') infirmière = nurse
6) cher	expensive		bon marché = cheap
7) fort	strong		faible = weak *febla*
8) court *et fem.*	short		long = long *feb. longue*
9) merci	thank you		de rien = you're welcome; s'il vous plaît = please *je vous en prie you are welcome*
10) Qu'est-ce qu'il y a? *aveque il e a*	What's the matter?	Qu'est-ce qui ne va pas? = What's wrong?	
11) Vous comprenez?	Do you understand? *ju ne comprapond pas*		
12) gentil	nice	sympa, extra = great; merveilleux = wonderful, marvel-lous; charmant = charming, lovely; chouette = swell	épouvantable = dreadful; horrible = horrible; affreux = awful; moche = crummy; dégueulasse = lousy
13) bête	stupid	stupide = dumb	intelligent = intelligent; malin = clever
14) gros	fat		mince = thin

grosse - fem.

Leçon 3/Lesson 3

Est-ce que c'est une boîte blanche?	=	Is it a white box?
Oui, c'est une boîte blanche.	=	Yes, it is a white box.
Non, ce n'est pas une boîte blanche.	=	No, it isn't a white box.

careful! → — 'un' (masculine) and 'une' (feminine) = a
— in general, place the adjective after the noun

Qu'est-ce que c'est?	=	What is it?
C'est une boîte blanche.	=	It's a white box.

1 **(un)** — 2 **(deux)** — 3 **(trois)** — 4 **(quatre)** — 5 **(cinq)**

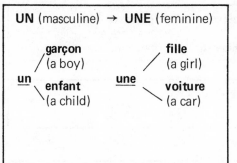

UN (masculine) → UNE (feminine)	ADJECTIVES
	masculine
garçon (a boy) / fille (a girl) / un enfant (a child) \ une voiture (a car) \	un livre **noir** (a black book)
	un stylo **vert** (a green pen)
	feminine
	une porte **bleue** (a blue door)
	une voiture **rouge** (a red car)

careful! — in general, don't forget to add an 'e' to adjectives to form the feminine. If the noun is feminine, the adjective is always feminine.

translate:

1) Is it a black pen?
2) Is it a blue telephone?
3) Is she a young nurse?
4) Is it an expensive watch?
5) Is it an interesting book?
6) It's a dirty table.
7) It's an easy lesson.
8) Is it a cheap car?

Est-ce que ce sont <u>des</u> voitures chères?	= Are they expensive cars?
Oui, ce sont <u>des</u> voitures chères.	= Yes, they are expensive cars.
Non, ce ne sont pas <u>des</u> voitures chères.	= No, they aren't expensive cars.

QU'EST-CE QUE C'EST?	= What are they?
Ce sont <u>des</u> voitures chères.	= They are expensive cars.

SINGULAR	PLURAL
<u>un</u> **homme** (a man)	→ <u>des</u> **homme<u>s</u>** (some men)
<u>un</u> **homme fort** (a strong man)	→ <u>des</u> **homme<u>s</u> fort<u>s</u>** (some strong men)
<u>une</u> **chaise** (a chair)	→ <u>des</u> **chaise<u>s</u>** (some chairs)
<u>une</u> **chaise rouge** (a red chair)	→ <u>des</u> **chaise<u>s</u> rouge<u>s</u>** (some red chairs)

careful! — remember that most plurals are usually formed by adding an 's'
to the noun, with certain exceptions (animal → anim<u>aux</u>,
chapeau → chapeaux, etc)
— do not pronounce the final 's' or 'x'
— if the noun is plural, the adjective is always plural
— those adjectives which end in 's' or 'x' do not change for the
plural

Est-ce que ce sont de jolis chats?	= Are they pretty cats?
Oui, ce sont de jolis chats.	= Yes, they're pretty cats.
Non, ce ne sont pas de jolis chats.	= No, they aren't pretty cats.

careful! — 'des' generally becomes 'de' when the adjective is in front of the noun (des voitures chères *but* de petites voitures)
— adjectives are generally placed after the noun, but the following are generally placed before:

beau = beautiful	**jeune** = young	**mauvais** = bad
bon = good	**joli** = pretty	**petit** = small
gros = big	**long** = long	**vieux** = old

put in the plural:

example: une voiture → des voitures rouges

1) un joli livre
2) un petit garçon
3) une femme intéressante
4) un beau garçon
5) un jeune chien
6) une leçon stupide
7) un mauvais médecin
8) une infirmière moche
9) une table noire
10) un téléphone blanc

11) un crayon bleu
12) un réveil rouge
13) un gros chat
14) un gosse mince
15) un enfant difficile
16) un mur sale
17) un vieux manteau
18) un bon gâteau
19) une boîte laide
20) un petit stylo

13

give the affirmative and negative answers, then give the singular form of each question:

---

example: Est-ce que les murs sont blancs?
Oui, les murs sont blancs.
Non, les murs ne sont pas blancs.
Est-ce que le mur est blanc?

---

1) Est-ce que les filles sont jeunes?
2) Est-ce que les manteaux sont noirs?
3) Est-ce que les gâteaux sont durs?
4) Est-ce que les chiens sont sous la table?
5) Est-ce que les hommes sont riches?
6) Est-ce que les leçons sont dures?
7) Est-ce que les portes sont noires?
8) Est-ce que nous sommes ici?
9) Est-ce que les crayons sont blancs?
10) Est-ce que les montres sont chères?

CONTRAIRES/OPPOSITES 2

1) **J'ai froid** (I'm cold)	≠	**très chaud/chaud** (hot/warm)
2) **Mon manteau est neuf/nouveau** (My coat's new)	≠	**vieux** (old)
3) **La règle est longue** (The ruler's long)	≠	**courte** (short)
4) **La voiture est rapide/va vite** (The car's fast/quick)	≠	**lente** (slow)
5) **Tu es gentil** (You're nice/kind)	≠	**méchant/vilain** (mean/nasty)
6) **Le pain est dur** (The bread's hard)	≠	**mou/doux** (soft)
7) **Le gâteau est bon** (The cake's good)	≠	**mauvais** (bad)
8) **Tu es en avance** (You're early)	≠	**en retard** (late)
9) **Lundi est avant mardi** (Monday is before Tuesday)	≠	**après** (after)
10) **Le restaurant est près** (The restaurant's near)	≠	**loin** (far)

translate:

a   1) Mardi est après lundi.
    2) Tu es en retard.
    3) La jeune fille est belle.
    4) La voiture bleue est vieille.
    5) La table rouge est loin.
    6) Le gâteau est mou, mais il est mauvais.

b   1) The man's interesting and the woman's nice.
    2) You're early and I'm late.
    3) The restaurant's good.
    4) You're mean and she is too.
    5) The book's difficult and the lessons are hard.
    6) The guy isn't old and the broad's young.

VOCABULAIRE/VOCABULARY

	translation	synonym/ associated	opposite/ associated
1) (le) chien	dog		(le) chat = cat, (la) souris = mouse
2) (la) chaise	chair		(la) table = table
3) (le) mur	wall		
4) (le) téléphone	telephone		
5) (le) stylo	pen	(le) crayon = pencil	
6) (la) montre	watch	(le) réveil = clock	
7) (la) porte	door		
8) près	near	à côté de = next to	loin = far
9) noir	black		blanc = white
10) sur	on	en, dans = in	sous = under
11) (le) livre	book	(la) page = page	
12) (l') homme	man	(le) mec, (le) type = guy, fellow	(la) femme = woman, (la) nana = broad
13) (le) garçon	boy		(la) fille = girl
14) (l') enfant	child	(le) gosse = kid, (le) bébé = baby	

Leçon 4/Lesson 4

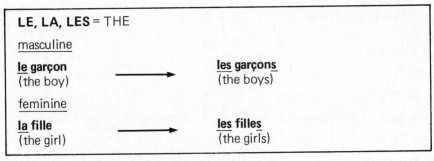

LE, LA, LES = THE

masculine

le garçon
(the boy)

──────────▶

les garçons
(the boys)

feminine

la fille
(the girl)

──────────▶

les filles
(the girls)

careful! — the plural of both 'le' and 'la' is 'les'
— in front of a vowel or a silent 'h', 'le' and 'la' become 'l''
(example: l'ami, l'hôpital, l'après-midi, l'homme)

Est-ce que < **le chien** / **la chienne**   **est** < **blanc?** / **blanche?**   = Is the dog white?

Oui, < **le chien** / **la chienne**   **est** < **blanc.** / **blanche.**   = Yes, the dog's white.

Non, < **le chien** / **la chienne**   **n'est pas** < **blanc.** / **blanche.**   = No, the dog isn't white.

6 **(six)** — 7 **(sept)** — 8 **(huit)** — 9 **(neuf)** — 10 **(dix)**

18

give the singular and plural negative answers:

example: Est-ce que le chat est noir?
Non, le chat n'est pas noir.
Non, les chats ne sont pas noirs.

1) Est-ce que la robe est bon marché?
2) Est-ce que le sac est sur la table?
3) Est-ce que le type est jeune?
4) Est-ce que la femme est grosse?
5) Est-ce que la leçon est difficile?
6) Est-ce que la chemise est noire?
7) Est-ce que je suis jeune?
8) Est-ce que la veste est neuve?
9) Est-ce que le mouchoir est sale?
10) Est-ce que la jupe est courte?

IL Y A = THERE IS, THERE ARE

Est-ce qu'il y a une femme ici?	= Is there a woman here?
Oui, il y a une femme ici.	= Yes, there is a woman here.
Non, il n'y a pas de femme ici.	= No, there is no woman here.
Est-ce qu'il y a quatre femmes ici?	= Are there four women here?
Oui, il y a quatre femmes ici.	= Yes, there are four women here.
Non, il n'y a pas quatre femmes ici.	= No, there aren't four women here.

---

translate:

a 1) Il y a deux chapeaux sur la chaise.
   2) Il y a un manteau à côté de Jane.
   3) Il y a quatre sacs ici.
   4) Il y a deux vieux hommes là.

b 1) There's a red dress on the chair.
   2) There's a baby next to the woman.
   3) There are five old sweaters here.
   4) There's a blue shirt under the table.

QUELLE HEURE EST-IL?	= What time is it?
Il est deux heures	= It's two o'clock
Il est deux heures moins vingt	= It's twenty to two
Il est deux heures dix	= It's ten past two
Il est deux heures trente	= It's two thirty
Il est deux heures et demie	= It's half past two

careful! — 'neuf heures et quart' = a quarter-past nine
        — 'neuf heures moins le quart' = a quarter to nine

translate:

a   1) Il est huit heures moins le quart.
      2) Il est une heure et demie.
      3) Il est trois heures et quart.
      4) Il est deux heures.
      5) Il est cinq heures et demie.

b   1) It's half past two.
      2) It's four thirty.
      3) It's a quarter past eight.
      4) It's six o'clock.
      5) It's ten to five.

SOME IRREGULAR ADJECTIVES

masculine	→ feminine	masculine	→ feminine
beau (beautiful)	→ **belle**	**gros** (big)	→ **grosse**
blanc (white)	→ **blanche**	**heureux** (happy)	→ **heureuse**
bon (good)	→ **bonne**	**long** (long)	→ **longue**
cher (expensive)	→ **chère**	**malheureux** (unhappy)	→ **malheureuse**
dernier (last)	→ **dernière**	**neuf** (new)	→ **neuve**
doux (soft)	→ **douce**	**nouveau** (new)	→ **nouvelle**
faux (false)	→ **fausse**	**premier** (first)	→ **première**
favori (favourite)	→ **favorite**	**vieux** (old)	→ **vieille**
gentil (kind)	→ **gentille**		

fill in the correct form of the adjectives:

de (beau) . . . jupes
de (gentil) . . . filles
une voiture (blanc) . . .
une (gros) . . . nana
un (bon) . . . gâteau
des filles (doux) . . .
des montres (cher) . . .
les bottes (neuf) . . .
une fille (heureux) . . .
la montre (faux) . . .

une (long) . . . table
de (vieux) . . . robes
la (premier) . . . porte
un enfant (malheureux) . . .
la (dernier) . . . page
une (nouveau) . . . leçon
la (beau) . . . veste
le livre (favori) . . .
de (vieux) . . . gants
les souris (blanc) . . .

VOCABULAIRE/VOCABULARY

	translation	synonym/ associated	opposite/ associated
1) (la) taille	size		
2) /aujourd-'hui /ce soir	/today/tonight		hier soir = last night
3) (la) chaussure	shoe	(la) chaussette = sock, (la) pantoufle = slipper	(la) botte = boot
4) /qui/où/quand?	/who?/where? /when?	quoi? = what?	
5) (le) chapeau	hat		(le) manteau = coat
6) (la) robe	dress	(la) jupe = skirt	
7) (la) chemise	shirt	(le) chemisier = blouse	
8) (la) veste	jacket	(le) complet, (le) tailleur = suit	
9) (le) pantalon	slacks, trousers	(les) jeans = jeans	
10) (le) sac	bag	(le) sac à main = handbag/(US) purse, (les) gants = gloves	
11) Comment vous appelez-vous?	What's your name?	Quel est votre nom?	
12) (le) pull	sweater	(le) col roulé = a turtle-neck, (le) pull-over = pullover	
13) (le) foulard	scarf	(le) mouchoir = handkerchief	
14) De quelle couleur est-ce?	What colour is it?		

Leçon 5/Lesson 5

POSSESSIVE ADJECTIVES

mon, ma, mes	=	my
ton, ta, tes **votre, vos**	=	your
son, sa, ses	=	his, her, its
notre, nos	=	our
leur, leurs	=	their

careful! — this is not so difficult as it seems: just find out WHAT is owned and not WHO owns it: (example: <u>mon</u> manteau (my coat), <u>sa</u> table (his/her table), <u>ta</u> soeur (your sister), <u>ses</u> chaussures (his/her shoes)
— remember to use 'ton', 'ta', 'tes' for family, friends.

Est-ce que c'est <u>ton</u> manteau?	=	Is it <u>your</u> coat?
Oui, c'est <u>mon</u> manteau.	=	Yes, it's <u>my</u> coat.
Non, ce n'est pas <u>mon</u> manteau.	=	No, it isn't <u>my</u> coat.

À qui est ce manteau?	=	<u>Whose</u> coat is it?
C'est <u>mon</u> manteau.	=	It's <u>my</u> coat.
Ce n'est pas <u>mon</u> manteau.	=	It isn't <u>my</u> coat.

translate:

a
1) Les gosses sont paresseux.
2) Son vélo est à côté de ma voiture.
3) Votre manteau est affreux.
4) Notre bouteille est vieille.
5) Ton cou est long et sale.
6) Leurs vêtements sont bon marché et jolis aussi.

b
1) Are they your cars?
2) Her umbrella's pretty.
3) Sunday is my favourite day.
4) His eyes are beautiful but his feet are ugly.
5) Our hands are dirty.
6) Their raincoats are old.

VOCABULAIRE/VOCABULARY

	translation	synonym/ associated	opposite/ associated
1) devant	in front of		derrière = behind
2) (la) voiture	car	(le) vélo, (la) bicyclette = bicycle	
3) (la) bouteille	bottle	(le) verre = glass	
4) (les) vêtements	clothes		
5) c'est vrai	that's right	c'est ça = that's it	ce n'est pas vrai = that isn't right
6) c'est l'heure	time's up	c'est tout = that's all	
7) continuez!	go on!	allez-y! continuez! = go ahead!	attendez une minute! = wait a minute!
8) (la) fênetre	window		
9) /(le) parapluie /(l')imperméable	/umbrella/raincoat		
10) (le) dimanche	Sunday	(le) lundi, mardi, mercredi, jeudi, vendredi, samedi	
11) paresseux	lazy		
12) (la) tête	head	(le) visage = face, (le) cou = neck	
13) (les) yeux	eyes	(un) oeil = an eye, (le) nez = nose, (les) oreilles = ears	
14) (la) main	hand	(le) bras = arm, (le) doigt = finger, (la) jambe = leg, (le) pied = foot, (le) doigt de pied = toe	

Leçon 6/Lesson 6

POSSESSIVE PRONOUNS

le(s) mien(s), la (les) mienne(s)	=	mine
le(s) tien(s), la(les) tienne(s) **le, la(les) vôtre(s)**	=	yours
le(s) sien(s), la(les) sienne(s)	=	her, his, its
le, la(les) nôtre(s)	=	ours
le, la(les) leur(s)	=	theirs

A QUI EST CE MANTEAU?	=	Whose coat is it?
C'est son manteau.	=	It's her/his coat.
C'est le sien.	=	It's hers/his.

EST-CE QUE C'EST <u>TA</u> VOITURE?	=	Is it <u>your</u> car?
Oui, c'est <u>ma</u> voiture.	=	Yes, it's <u>my</u> car.
Oui, c'est <u>la mienne</u>.	=	Yes, it's <u>mine</u>.

EST-CE QUE CE SONT <u>SES</u> CHAUSSURES?	=	Are they <u>his/her</u> shoes?
Oui, ce sont <u>ses</u> chaussures.	=	Yes, they're <u>his/her</u> shoes.
Oui, ce sont <u>les siennes</u>.	=	Yes, they're <u>his/hers</u>.

give the possessive pronoun:

> example: Est-ce que c'est <u>mon</u> pull?
>   Oui, c'est <u>le mien</u>.

1) Est-ce que c'est ton vélo? — Oui, c'est . . . . . .
2) Est-ce que c'est leur bouteille? — Oui, c'est . . . . . .
3) Est-ce que ce sont nos parapluies? — Oui, ce sont . . . . . .
4) Est-ce que c'est son visage? — Oui, c'est . . . . . .
5) Est-ce que ce sont ses doigts? — Oui, ce sont . . . . . .
6) Est-ce que ce sont tes chiens? — Oui, ce sont . . . . . .
7) Est-ce que ce sont mes vêtements? — Oui, ce sont . . . . . .
8) Est-ce que ce sont ses jambes? — Oui, ce sont . . . . . .
9) Est-ce que c'est notre voiture? — Oui, c'est . . . . . .
10) Est-ce que c'est votre veste? — Oui, c'est . . . . . .
11) Est-cè que c'est son pull? — Oui, c'est . . . . . .
12) Est-ce que ce sont ses chaussures? — Oui, ce sont . . . . . .
13) Est-ce que c'est de votre faute? — Oui, c'est de . . . . . .

translate:

a 1) Ta bouche est petite et la mienne aussi.
   2) Est-ce que c'est votre avion? — Oui, c'est le mien.
   3) Est-ce que c'est sa voiture? — Non, ce n'est pas la sienne.
   4) Est-ce que c'est notre bateau? — Non, ce n'est pas le nôtre.
   5) Notre école est jolie et la leur aussi.
   6) Leur métro est très sale mais le nôtre est propre.

b 1) Is it your train? — Yes, it's mine.
   2) Are they his boxes? — Yes, they're his.
   3) Our teeth are dirty and yours are too.
   4) Her feet aren't hot, but mine are.
   5) Their teacher is nice but ours isn't.
   6) Your class is difficult and mine is too.

VOCABULAIRE/VOCABULARY

	translation	synonym/ associated	opposite/ associated
1) (la) bouche	mouth	(les) dents = teeth	
2) pourquoi?	why?		parce que = because
3) Comment l'épelez vous?	How do you spell it?	Comment ça s'écrit? = How do you write it?	
4) Est-ce que vous pouvez répéter, s'il vous plaît?	Would you repeat it, please?		
5) avec	with		sans = without
6) (la) faute	mistake	(l') erreur	
7) (par) (l')avion	(by) plane	(le) bateau = boat	
8) (le) train	train		
9) (le) métro	subway, underground		
10) fou	crazy	dingue = nuts	
11) d'accord!	all right!	O.K. = O.K., ça va	ça ne va pas = it's not O.K.
12) (la) leçon	lesson	(les) devoirs = homework	
13) (l')étudiant	student	(l')élève = pupil, (l') école = school, (le) professeur = teacher, (le) cours = course, (la) classe = class	
14) (le) flic	cop	(l')agent de police, (le) gendarme = policeman	

30

Leçon 7/Lesson 7

POSSESSION

La voiture de Pierre	=	Peter's car
Les chaussures de Marie	=	Mary's shoes
Les livres des étudiants	=	The students' books

careful! — Wow! finally, a construction which is easier in French than in English

---

le livre du garçon — **de + le** → **du**
(the boy's book)

la voiture de la fille — **de + la** → **de la**
(the girl's car)

les livres des garçons
(the boys' books)
} — **de + les** → **des**
les voitures des filles
(the girls' cars)

les devoirs de l'étudiant — **de + l'** → **de l'**
(the student's homework)

---

careful! — 'de le' is wrong!

11 **(onze)** — 12 **(douze)** — 13 **(treize)** — 14 **(quatorze)** — 15 **(quinze)**

fill in appropriately with **de, du, de la, des** or **de l'**

1) la bouche . . . fille
2) les mains . . . gosses
3) la jupe . . . femme
4) les yeux . . . enfant
5) les vêtements . . . fille
6) le plafond . . . classe
7) le nez . . . Pierre
8) les jours . . . mois
9) les bottes . . . filles
10) la bouteille . . . père
11) l'imperméable . . . professeur
12) la leçon . . . étudiant
13) les mois . . . année
14) les chaussures . . . agent de police
15) le métro . . . Paris
16) les dents . . . chien
17) le nom . . . rue
18) les papiers . . . voiture
19) la maison . . . famille
20) les jambes . . . bébé
21) la couleur . . . pantalon
22) les oreilles . . . souris
23) l'imperméable . . . médecin
24) le chemisier . . . infirmière

translate:

a 1) Les yeux de Jane sont bleus.
   2) Le sac de la femme est grand.
   3) Le parapluie d'Anne est près du mur.
   4) La voiture de Pierre est devant la porte.
   5) Ton chat est sur la table et le mien est sur la chaise.
   6) Le livre du gosse est sous son bras mais le mien est à côté de moi.

b 1) Anne's bike is green.
   2) The teacher's students are lazy.
   3) John's school is near mine.
   4) My sister's teeth are dirty.
   5) The girl's mouth is beautiful.
   6) My father's feet are big.

```
┌─────────────────────────────────────────────────────────────┐
│  CE ... = THIS            CE ... LÀ = THAT                    │
│  ce garçon = this boy     ce garçon-là = that boy             │
│  cette fille = this girl  cette fille-là = that girl          │
└─────────────────────────────────────────────────────────────┘
```

careful! — 'ce' becomes 'cet' before a silent 'h' or a vowel (example: cet homme, cet enfant)

translate:

a 1) Cet avion est rapide, mais ce bateau-là est lent.
   2) Cette fille est folle.
   3) Ce professeur n'est pas bon.
   4) Ce livre-là est affreux.

b 1) That man is my father.
   2) This house is mine.
   3) This winter is lousy.
   4) This sweater's mine but that turtleneck's yours.

1) **Cette rue est dangereuse**   ≠   **sûre**
   (this street's dangerous)   (safe)

2) **Qui est le premier?**   ≠   **dernier**
   (who is first?)   (last)

3) **Une voiture neuve n'est pas bon marché** ≠ **chère**
   (a new car isn't cheap)   (expensive)

4) **La boîte est lourde**   ≠   **légère**
   (the box's heavy)   (light)

5) **Pierre est en haut**   ≠   **en bas**
   (Peter's upstairs)   (downstairs)

6) **La maison est vide**   ≠   **pleine**
   (the house's empty)   (full)

7) **Le gâteau est sucré**   ≠   **amer/aigre**
   (the cake's sweet)   (bitter/sour)

8) **L'avenue est étroite**   ≠   **large**
   (the avenue's narrow)   (wide/broad)

9) **Le livre est mince**   ≠   **épais**
   (the book's thin)   (thick)

10) **Le mur est haut**   ≠   **bas**
    (the wall's high)   (low)

translate:

a   1) La chaise n'est pas lourde et la table non plus.
      2) Le verre est plein et la bouteille aussi.
      3) Est-ce que tu es en haut?
      4) Est-ce qu'une maison neuve est chère?
      5) Je ne suis pas le premier et toi non plus.
      6) Le bateau est large mais l'avion ne l'est pas.

b   1) There aren't many safe avenues in Paris.
      2) My book isn't thick but it's cheap.
      3) My sister isn't downstairs and my mother isn't either.
      4) There are lots of people in this street.
      5) My bike's low and yours is too.
      6) This candy isn't bitter but it's hard.

VOCABULAIRE/VOCABULARY

	translation	synonym/associated	opposite/associated
1) /(le) jour, /(la) semaine	/day,/week		
2) /(le) mois, /(l')année	/month,/year		
3) (le) printemps	spring	(l')été = summer, (l')automme = autumn, (l')hiver = winter	
4) janvier	January	février, mars, avril, mai, juin, juillet, août, septembre, octobre, novembre, décembre	
5) (le) matin	(in the) morning	(l')après-midi = (in the) afternoon, (la) nuit = (at) night, (le) soir = (in the) evening	
6) beaucoup de	a lot of, plenty of	des tas de = lots of, trop = too much, too many	un peu = a bit, a little, quelques = a few
7) aujourd'hui	today	demain = tomorrow	hier = yesterday
8) (la) personne	person		des gens = des personnes = people
9) (la) famille	family	un parent = a relative, les parents (père et mère) = parents	
10) (le) père	father		(la) mère = mother
11) (la) soeur	sister		(le) frère = brother
12) (la) maison	house, home	(l')appartement = apartment, flat	
13) Qu'est-ce que ça veut dire?	What does it mean?	(le) sens = the meaning	
14) /tout,/quelque chose, /quelqu'un	/everything, /something, /someone	tous = all, tout le monde = everyone	rien = nothing, personne = no one

AVOIR = TO HAVE

j'<u>ai</u> ≠ je n'ai pas *Ju ne pas*		=	I have ≠ I don't have
tu <u>as</u> ≠ tu n'<u>as pas</u> *a* *tu na*			you have ≠ you don't have

il   il
elle } <u>a</u> ≠ elle } **n'a pas**
~~ça~~   ~~ça~~

he   he
she } has ≠ she } doesn't have
it   it

navon
nous <u>avons</u> ≠ nous **n'avons pas**   we have ≠ we don't have

havey
vous <u>avez</u> ≠ vous **n'avez pas**   you have ≠ you don't have

lizont
ils   ils
    } <u>ont</u> ≠   } **n'ont pas**   they have ≠ they don't have
elles   elles

careful! — don't forget the use of the French present for our present perfect
(j'<u>ai</u> ma voiture depuis cinq ans = I'<u>ve had</u> my car for five years)

ils sont

Est-ce qu'elle <u>a</u> un chien?	Does she have a dog?
Oui, elle <u>a</u> un chien.	Yes, she has a dog.
Non, elle <u>n'a pas</u> de chien.	Non, she doesn't have a dog.

16 **(seize)** — 17 **(dix-sept)** — 18 **(dix-huit)** — 19 **(dix-neuf)** — 20 **(vingt)**

translate and then put into the French interrogative:

a 1) Le professeur a beaucoup d'élèves stupides.
  2) Elle a cinq couteaux, trois fourchettes et huit cuillers.
  3) Ils ont quelques cols roulés.
  4) Nous n'avons pas une grande maison.
  5) Ma soeur a deux enfants.
  6) Une heure a 60 minutes.

translate only:

b 1) Do you have nine knives?
  2) Each day has 24 hours.
  3) Does she have a napkin?
  4) This restaurant doesn't have pretty plates.
  5) I'm sure the school's very good.
  6) Do you have an umbrella with you?

ADVERBS, etc — List 1

1)	**à peu près**	nearly
	presque	almost
2)	**au moins**	at least
3)	**bientôt**	soon
4)	**de toutes façons**	at any rate
	de toutes manières	anyway
	en tous cas	in any case
5)	**d'habitude**	usually
	généralement	generally
6)	**parfois/quelquefois**	sometimes
7)	**rarement**	rarely, seldom
8)	**sauf**	except
9)	**souvent**	often
	fréquemment	frequently
10)	**toujours**	always

translate:

a 1) Je suis vraiment en retard.
   2) Elle est souvent fatiguée le soir.
   3) Tu as presque dix francs et Jane aussi.
   4) Je suis parfois très heureuse.
   5) Nous sommes toujours gentils avec nos parents.
   6) Tout est cher sauf ce gâteau-là.

b 1) They have at least twenty francs.
   2) We usually eat at home except on Sundays.
   3) She seldom has her raincoat with her.
   4) We almost have fifteen dollars.
   5) The restaurant generally has good bread.
   6) Anyway my teacher's very nice.

AVOIR	→ TO BE
j'ai ... ans *show*	I'm ... years old
j'ai chaud/j'ai froid	I'm hot/I'm cold
j'ai de la chance *h faan*	I'm lucky
j'ai faim/j'ai soif *swaf*	I'm hungry/I'm thirsty
j'ai peur	I'm afraid
j'ai raison/j'ai tort	I'm right/I'm wrong
j'ai sommeil *so-may*	I'm sleepy

translate:

1) I'm not hungry, but I'm thirsty.
2) In any case I'm afraid.
3) I'm almost ten years old.
4) I'm not hot but I'm not cold either.
5) I'm sure you're right.
6) I'm not wrong and I am glad!
7) You're lucky!
8) Are you sleepy?

te llement – really   as in really thirsty
    telmon
            j'ai tellement soif

translate:

a 1) Je suis pressée et Jane aussi.
    2) Mon père est rarement au travail à sept heures du matin.
    3) D'habitude nous avons très faim le soir.
    4) De toutes façons, tu n'es pas méchant.
    5) Ma mère et mon père ne sont pas toujours sympas.
    6) Ils ont souvent froid en février dans leur maison.
    7) Je suis très occupée à midi.
    8) Elle est seule une heure tous les jours.

b 1) Are you cold?
    2) You're always very lucky.
    3) I'm very afraid, but she isn't.
    4) My sister's very sleepy and he is, too.
    5) I'm sure you're wrong.
    6) Anyway you're always right.
    7) I'm usually at home at 8 o'clock.
    8) Whose turn is it?

VOCABULAIRE/VOCABULARY

	translation	synonym/ associated	opposite/ associated
1) à midi	at noon		à minuit = at midnight
2) une heure	an hour	une seconde = a second, une minute = a minute, un quart d'heure = a quarter of an hour, une demi-heure = half an hour	
3) occupé	busy		libre = free
4) pressé	in a hurry		
5) à l'école	at school	au travail = at work, à la maison = chez moi = at home, à huit heures du soir = at eight p.m.	
6) A qui est-ce la tour?	Whose turn is it?		
7) certain	certain	sûr = sure	douteux = doubtful
8) tous les (jours)	every (day)	chaque = each	
9) seul	alone		
10) (le) couteau	knife	(la) fourchette = fork, (la) cuiller = spoon	
11) (la) serviette (de table)	napkin		
12) (le) restaurant	restaurant	(le) menu = menu	
13) (l') assiette	plate	(la) tasse = cup	
14) (le) pain	bread	(le) beurre = butter	

44

Leçon 9/Lesson 9

The three groups of French verbs end in ER, IR and RE

VERBS ENDING IN **ER**

PRESENT TENSE — **travailler**

je travaille ≠ **je ne travaille pas**	I work, I'm working ≠ I don't work, I'm not working
tu travailles ≠ **tu ne travailles pas**	you work, you're working ≠ you don't work, you aren't working
il ⎫ **il** ⎫ **elle** ⎬ **travaille** ≠ **elle** ⎬ **ne travaille pas** **on** ⎭ **on** ⎭	he ⎫ she ⎬ works, is working ≠ one ⎭ he ⎫ she ⎬ doesn't work, isn't working one ⎭
nous travaillons ≠ **nous ne travaillons pas**	we work, we're working ≠ we don't work, we aren't working
vous travaillez ≠ **vous ne travaillez pas**	you work, you're working ≠ you don't work, you aren't working
ils travaillent ≠ **ils ne travaillent pas**	they work, they're working ≠ they don't work, they aren't working

careful! — ON is frequently used, meaning 'one', 'they', 'you' or 'we'
— note the extensive use of the French present:
  — for an action one is in the midst of doing (je travaille maintenant = I'm working now)
  — for an action which is repeated (je travaille souvent = I often work)
  — for an action begun in the past and still continuing, and where we use our present perfect (je travaille depuis deux heures = I've been working for two hours)

EST-CE QUE VOUS TRAVAILLEZ SOUVENT LE SOIR?	= Do you often work at night?
Oui, je travaille souvent le soir.	= Yes, I often work at night.
Non, je ne travaille pas souvent le soir.	= No, I don't often work at night.

give French affirmative and negative answers:

> example: Do you work at school?
> Oui, je travaille à l'école.
> Non, je ne travaille pas à l'école.

a   1) Do children usually play every day?
      2) Does your father work at home?
      3) Does it often snow in summer?
      4) Do children ask a lot of questions?
      5) Do we often eat in a restaurant?
      6) Does she generally get dressed alone?

translate only:

b   1) Je mange tous les jours beaucoup de gâteaux.
      2) Je ne travaille pas souvent avec son frère.
      3) Tu poses trop de questions.
      4) En ce moment il ne neige pas.
      5) Ma soeur s'habille seule.
      6) Nous parlons beaucoup ensemble.

IRREGULAR VERBS ENDING IN 'ER'

ACHETER (to buy)	= j'achète tu achètes il achète nous achetons vous achetez ils achètent	**ESPÉRER** (to hope)	= j'espère tu espères il espère nous espérons vous espérez ils espèrent
ALLER (to go)	= je vais tu vas il va nous allons vous allez ils vont	**JETER** (to throw)	= je jette tu jettes il jette nous jetons vous jetez ils jettent
COMMENCER (to begin)	= je commence tu commences il commence nous commençons vous commencez ils commencent	**MANGER** (to eat)	= je mange tu manges il mange nous mangeons vous mangez ils mangent
ENVOYER (to send)	= j'envoie tu envoies il envoie nous envoyons vous envoyez ils envoient	**PRÉFÉRER** (to prefer)	= je préfère tu préfères il préfère nous préférons vous préférez ils préfèrent

translate:

a   1) Est-ce que tu y vas aujourd'hui?
    2) Nous mangeons trop de gâteaux.
    3) Mes enfants jettent souvent leurs vêtements sur la chaise.
    4) J'espère beaucoup manger au restaurant ce soir.
    5) Mes parents achètent toujours des jouets bon marché.
    6) S'il te plaît, envoie-moi un nouveau jeu.

b   1) We rarely go to school at seven o'clock.
    2) We're beginning to understand the question.
    3) We usually eat very early.
    4) They're sending a lot of toys to their friends' kids.
    5) He's buying a new car.
    6) She hopes to have another dog soon.

```
┌─────────────────────────────────────────────────────────────┐
│  QUI? = WHO?                                                  │
│                                                               │
│  Qui est ici?                    =  Who is here?              │
│  Qui commence?                   =  Who is beginning?         │
└─────────────────────────────────────────────────────────────┘
```

```
┌─────────────────────────────────────────────────────────────┐
│  QUE? = WHAT?                                                 │
│                                                               │
│  Que voyez-vous?                 =  What do you see?          │
│  Que penses-tu?                  =  What do you think?        │
└─────────────────────────────────────────────────────────────┘
```

translate:

1) What are you asking?
2) Who's eating with you tonight?
3) Who's playing with your sister?
4) What are they buying?

```
┌─────────────────────────────────────────────────────────────┐
│  A + . . . = TO the                                          │
│                                                               │
│  j'écris au professeur =          à + le = au                │
│  I'm writing to the teacher                                   │
│                                                               │
│  j'écris à la femme =             à + la = à la              │
│  I'm writing to the woman                                     │
│                                                               │
│  j'écris aux enfants =            à + les = aux              │
│  I'm writing to the children                                  │
└─────────────────────────────────────────────────────────────┘
```

careful! — envoyer à = to send to; parler à = to speak to; montrer à = to
          show to; donner à = to give to
          Exception: penser à = to think about

translate:

1) Je parle à mon frère.
2) Je pense souvent à toi.
3) Je vais parfois au restaurant.
4) Montre ton nouveau vélo à ton père.

VOCABULAIRE/VOCABULARY

	translation	synonym/ associated	opposite/ associated
1) jouer	to play	(le) jeu = game, (le) jouet = toy	travailler = to work
2) /pleuvoir/neiger	/to rain/to snow	(la) pluie = rain, (la) neige = snow	(le) soleil = sun, ensoleillé = sunny
3) (le) tableau (noir)	blackboard	(la) craie = chalk	
4) plusieurs	several		
5) combien (de)?	how many?		
6) un/une autre	another	autre = other	
7) venir	to come		aller(à) = to go (to)
8) répondre	to answer		demander = to ask, poser une question = to ask a question
9) content	glad, pleased		
10) (la) question	question		(la) réponse = answer
11) manger	to eat	boire = to drink	
12) /s'habiller/se laver	/to get dressed /to get washed		
13) maintenant	now	en ce moment = at present	
14) prêt	ready		

Leçon 10/Lesson 10

VERBS ENDING IN **IR**

PRESENT TENSE — **choisir**

je choisis ≠ **je ne choisis pas**
I choose, I'm choosing ≠ I don't choose, I'm not choosing

tu choisis ≠ **tu ne choisis pas**
you choose, you're choosing ≠ you don't choose, you aren't choosing

il
elle } **choisit** ≠ **il elle** } **ne choisit pas**
on   **on**
he
she } chooses, is choosing ≠
one

he
she } doesn't choose, isn't choosing
one

nous choisissons ≠ **nous ne choisissons pas**
we choose, we're choosing ≠ we don't choose, we aren't choosing

vous choisissez ≠ **vous ne choisissez pas**
you choose, you're choosing ≠ you don't choose, you aren't choosing

ils
elles } **choisissent** ≠ **ils elles** } **ne choisissent pas**
they choose, they're choosing ≠ they don't choose, they aren't choosing

---

careful! — another very useful verb in this group: finir = to finish

---

EST-CE QU'ELLE CHOISIT TOUJOURS LA MÊME CHOSE?
Does she always choose the same thing?

Oui, elle choisit toujours la même chose. = Yes, she always chooses the same thing.

Non, elle ne choisit pas toujours la même chose. = No, she doesn't always choose the same thing.

---

translate:

1) Are they choosing a new house?
2) She's finishing her lunch.
3) We're choosing a new dog.
4) You're finishing before me.

```
┌─────────────────────────────────────────────────────────────────┐
│ QUI = WHO, WHICH, THAT — relative pronoun subject                 │
│                                                                   │
│ La femme qui est ici        =   the woman who is here             │
│                                          ⎧ which                  │
│ la voiture qui est dans la rue  =   the car ⎨ ─────  is in the street │
│                                          ⎩ that                   │
└─────────────────────────────────────────────────────────────────┘


┌─────────────────────────────────────────────────────────────────┐
│ QUE = WHO(M), WHICH, THAT — relative pronoun object               │
│ La femme que j'aime         =   the woman who(m) I love           │
│                                          ⎧ which                  │
│ la voiture que j'achète     =   the car  ⎨ ─────  I'm buying      │
│                                          ⎩ that                   │
└─────────────────────────────────────────────────────────────────┘
```

careful! — Before a vowel, **que** becomes **qu'** e.g. qu'il, qu'elle

```
┌─────────────────────────────────────────────────────────────────┐
│ examples:                                                         │
│   ⎧ Que voyez-vous?        =  ⎧ What are you seeing?              │
│   ⎨ Qui voyez-vous?        =  ⎨ Who are you looking at?           │
│   ⎩ Qui vous voit?         =  ⎩ Who is looking at you?            │
│                                                                   │
│   ⎧ Que manges-tu?         =  ⎧ What are you eating?              │
│   ⎨ Qui mange çà?          =  ⎨ Who eats that?                    │
│                                                                   │
│   ⎧ Qui sait?              =  ⎧ Who knows?                        │
│   ⎨ Que sait-il?           =  ⎨ What does he know?                │
│                                                                   │
│   ⎧ Le livre que je veux   =  ⎧ The book (which) I want           │
│   ⎨ Le livre qui est ici   =  ⎨ The book which (that) is here.    │
└─────────────────────────────────────────────────────────────────┘
```

translate:

a 1) Qui habite cette jolie maison?
    2) Que mets-tu dans ton sac?
    3) Qui te donne de l'argent toutes les semaines?
    4) Que savez-vous?
    5) Le professeur que je rencontre tous les jours est sympa.
    6) Les vêtements que Maman achète sont beaux.

b 1) Children who work too much are unhappy.
    2) The bike you're buying is expensive.
    3) The department store that you're looking for is a long way away
       [very far].
    4) I'm living in a house which is very pretty.
    5) You need money: it's on the table.
    6) The woman who is working in that store/shop is my aunt.

QUEL(S)?/QUELLE(S)? = WHICH?/WHAT?	
masculine	feminine
Quel garçon? = Which boy?	**Quelle fille?** = Which girl?
Quels garçons? = Which boys?	**Quelles filles?** = Which girls?

use the correct form of 'quel':

1) . . . chat?
2) . . . magasin?
3) . . . couteau?
4) . . . argent?
5) . . . beurre?
6) . . . jour?
7) . . . année?
8) . . . été?
9) . . . maison?
10) . . . rues?
11) . . . problèmes?
12) . . . parapluie?
13) . . . métro?
14) . . . étudiant?
15) . . . tête?
16) . . . chapeau?

17) . . . chaise?
18) . . . bicyclette?
19) . . . restaurant?
20) . . . film?
21) . . . mères?
22) . . . mois?
23) . . . printemps?
24) . . . personnes?
25) . . . grand magasin?
26) . . . bouteille?
27) . . . plafond?
28) . . . faute?
29) . . . leçon?
30) . . . flics?
31) . . . vêtements?
32) . . . pantalon?

VOCABULAIRE/VOCABULARY

	translation	synonym/ associated	opposite/ associated
1) (le) problème	problem	(la) difficulté = difficulty	
2) aller au cinéma	to go to the movies	(le) film = film	
3) payer	to pay		
4) vivre (à)	to live (in)	habiter (à)	
5) rencontrer	to meet		
6) trop (cher)	too (expensive)	assez = enough	pas assez = not . . . enough
7) dormir	to sleep	aller se coucher = to go to bed	
8) savoir (quelque chose)	to know (something)	connaître (quelqu'un) = to know (someone)	
9) (l') argent	money	(le) fric = 'bread'	
10) mettre	to put		
11) choisir	to choose		
12) prendre	to take		
13) (le) magasin	store, shop	(la) boutique = boutique, (le) grand magasin = department store	
14) (tous) les deux	both	ensemble = together	

Leçon 11/Lesson 11

VERBS ENDING IN **RE**

PRESENT TENSE — **attendre**

j'attends ≠ **je n'attends pas**	I wait, I'm waiting ≠ I don't wait, I'm not waiting
tu attends ≠ **tu n'attends pas**	you wait, you're waiting ≠ you don't wait, you aren't waiting
il **elle** } **attend** ≠ **elle** } **n'attend pas** **on**	he she } waits, is waiting ≠ one he she } doesn't wait, isn't waiting one
nous attendons ≠ **nous n'attendons pas**	we wait, we're waiting ≠ we don't wait, we aren't waiting
vous attendez ≠ **vous n'attendez pas**	you wait, you're waiting ≠ you don't wait, you aren't waiting
ils attendent ≠ **ils n'attendent pas**	they wait, they're waiting ≠ they don't wait, they aren't waiting

---

careful! — included in this group are some verbs ending in AÎTRE, OIR, and IR
— remember the use of the French present for an action begun in the past and still continuing: j'attends depuis deux heures = I've been waiting for two hours

---

EST-CE QUE VOUS M'ATTENDEZ SOUVENT?
Do you often wait for me?

Oui, je vous attends souvent	=	Yes, I often wait for you.
Non, je ne vous attends pas souvent	=	No, I don't often wait for you.

CONNAÎTRE = (to know)	je connais tu connais il connaît nous connaissons vous connaissez ils connaissent	**PARTIR** = (to leave)	je pars tu pars il part nous partons vous partez ils partent
COURIR = (to run)	je cours tu cours il court nous courons vous courez ils courent	**RÉPONDRE** = (to answer)	je réponds tu réponds il répond nous répondons vous répondez ils répondent
DORMIR = (to sleep)	je dors tu dors il dort nous dormons vous dormez ils dorment	**RIRE** = (to laugh)	je ris tu ris il rit nous rions vous riez ils rient
ÉCRIRE = (to write)	j'écris tu écris il écrit nous écrivons vous écrivez ils écrivent	**SENTIR** = (to feel)	je sens tu sens il sent nous sentons vous sentez ils sentent
FAIRE = (to do/make)	je fais tu fais il fait nous faisons vous faites ils font	**SORTIR** = (to go out)	je sors tu sors il sort nous sortons vous sortez ils sortent
OUVRIR = (to open)	j'ouvre tu ouvres il ouvre nous ouvrons vous ouvrez ils ouvrent	**VIVRE** = (to live)	je vis tu vis il vit nous vivons vous vivez ils vivent

translate:

a
1) Ne répondez pas maintenant.
2) Est-ce que tu connais mon frère? *do you know my brother*
3) Qu'est-ce que tu fais? *What is that you do?*
4) Je vis à Paris depuis deux ans. ~~I usually write my~~ *aunt*
5) Mes parents dorment ensemble. *my parents sleep together*
6) Il m'écrit souvent. *he always writes to me*
   to me

b
1) We're leaving this afternoon at 5 o'clock.
2) I usually write to my grandmother every week. *dabitu*
3) Why are you running? *porqua es shock*
4) I often go out without my parents. *sorty cours?*
5) Open the window, please. *ovre la fenetre*
6) Why are you laughing?
   Porqua est-ca tu re
   (est-ce que)

58

S'ASSEOIR (to sit down)	=	je m'assois tu t'assois il s'assoit nous nous asseyons vous <u>vous asseyez</u> ils s'assoient	**POUVOIR** (can/to be able to)	= je peux tu peux il peut nous pouvons vous pouvez ils peuvent
BOIRE (to drink)	=	je bois tu bois il boit nous buvons vous buvez ils boivent	**PRENDRE** (to take)	= je prends tu prends il prend nous prenons vous prenez ils prennent
COMPRENDRE (to understand)	=	<u>je comprends</u> tu comprends il comprend nous comprenons vous comprenez ils comprennent	**SAVOIR** (to know)	= je sais tu sais il sait nous savons vous savez ils savent
DIRE (to say/tell)	=	je dis tu dis il dit nous disons vous dites ils disent	**VENIR** (to come)	= je viens tu viens il vient nous venons vous venez ils viennent
LIRE (to read)	=	je lis tu lis il lit nous lisons vous lisez ils lisent	**VOIR** (to see)	= je vois tu vois il voit nous voyons vous voyez ils voient
METTRE (to put)	=	je mets tu mets il met nous mettons vous mettez ils mettent	**VOULOIR** (to want)	= je veux tu veux il veut nous voulons vous voulez ils veulent

Handwritten notes: asseyez / assoit / vous / sit down ; pron (beside tu prends) ; say (beside je sais) ; vo (beside il voit)

59

translate:

a
1) Je m'assois toujours à côté de mon copain. *to dinner lunch*
   I eat meat every day meat
2) Je mange presque toujours de la viande pour le déjeuner.
   I dont understand why you need this book
3) Je ne comprends pas pourquoi tu as besoin de ce livre.
4) Je vois mes amis tous les jours.
5) Je ne sais pas ma leçon.
6) Nous ne pouvons pas regarder la télévision ce soir.
   We are not able to look at the tv. in the
   Je vois mon amis tou le jour *this evening*

b
1) I want to see my friends every day.
2) Come and sit down next to me.
3) We drink a lot of milk every day. *nous bouyon beaucoup*
4) Put the chicken on the table. *mete le pouler a la de lait*
5) Tell me why you're late. *tu dit moi porqua retarde. taste.*
6) What book are you reading?
   Quel livre le tu
   est-ce tu lis

60

VOCABULAIRE/VOCABULARY

	translation	synonym/ associated	opposite/ associated
1) /(la) radio/(la) télévision	/radio/television		
2) je crois bien	I believe so, I guess so	j'espère bien = I hope so, je pense que oui = I think so	
3) avoir besoin de	to need		
4) seulement	only	juste = just, simplement = simply	
5) ça ne fait rien	it doesn't matter	cela n'a aucune importance = never mind	
6) une fois	once		deux fois = twice
7) (l')ami	friend	(le) copain = pal	(l')ennemi = enemy
8) marcher	to walk	aller se promener = to go for a walk	
9) (le) petit déjeuner	breakfast	(le) déjeuner = lunch	(le) dîner = dinner, supper
10) (le) repas	meal	(la) nourriture = food	
11) (la) viande	meat	(le) poulet = chicken, (le) steak = steak, (le) veau = veal, (l')agneau = lamb, (le) boeuf = beef	
12) parler avec/à	to talk with/to, to speak with/to		
13) vouloir	to want (to)	souhaiter = to wish	
14) sentir	to feel	avoir l'impression de = to have the feeling that	

61

Leçon 12/Lesson 12

> **IL FAUT** = (I, you, he, she, one, we, they) HAVE TO, MUST
>
> **Est-ce qu'il faut manger**   Do we have to/must we
> **tous les jours?**   eat everyday?
>
> **Oui, il faut manger tous les jours.**   Yes, we have to/must eat every day.

careful! — this is very much used in French

> **DEVOIR** = to have to/must/should
>
> | | | |
> |---|---|---|
> | **je dois** | = | I |
> | **tu dois** | = | you |
> | **il** **elle** } **doit** **on** | = | he she one } |
> | **nous devons** | = | we |
> | **vous devez** | = | you |
> | **ils** **elles** } **doivent** | = | they |
>
> have to/must/should

careful! — this is used, but less often

translate:

a   1) Il faut parler français.
      2) Nous ne devons pas parler en classe.
      3) Est-ce qu'il faut payer tout de suite?
      4) Tu ne dois pas boire trop de lait.
              to drink

b   1) We must eat every day.
      2) Do we have to leave now?
      3) You mustn't eat that.
      4) I'm hungry, we must buy something to eat.

Trop — too much much

ADVERBS, etc — List 2

1)	**à peine**	scarcely, hardly, barely
2)	**comme d'habitude**	as usual
3)	**déjà ≠ pas encore**	already ≠ not yet
4)	**enfin**	at last
5)	**entre**	between
6)	**environ**	about
7)	**jusqu'à**	until
8)	**peut-être**	perhaps, maybe
9)	**plus ou moins**	more or less
10)	**plutôt**	pretty
11)	**tout à fait**	quite
12)	**très**	very

translate:

a 1) J'ai à peine faim.
2) Le serveur est plutôt intelligent.
3) Entre les frites et les haricots verts, je veux des haricots verts.
4) Le poisson est peut-être bon ici.
5) Tu as tout à fait raison.
6) Je ne veux pas travailler jusqu'à six heures.

b 1) We hardly have enough bread for dinner.
2) I'm busy until three o'clock.
3) It doesn't matter, we have more or less enough money.
4) The waiter wants a big tip as usual.
5) How much does it cost about?
6) At last, the check/bill is here.

	translation	synonym/ associated	opposite/ associated
1) je n'ai plus faim	I'm full	je cale	j'ai faim = I'm hungry, je meurs de faim = I'm starving
2) saignant	rare	à point = medium	bien cuit = well done
3) (le) poisson	fish		
4) (la) pomme de terre	potato	(les) frites = French fries, (la) purée = mashed potatoes	
5) (la) soupe	soup	(le) bol = bowl	
6) (la) laitue	lettuce	(la) tomate = tomato, (la) salade = salad	
7) Combien est-ce?	How much is it?	Combien est-ce que ça coûte? = How much does it cost?	
8) (le) dessert	dessert	(le) gâteau = cake, (la) glace = ice cream, (le) parfum = flavour	
9) (l')addition	check, bill	(la) note	
10) /(le) lait/l'eau	/milk/water	(une) boisson = a drink	
11) /(le) pourboire /(le) garçon	/tip/waiter	(le) serveur, (la) serveuse = waitress	
12) des oeufs au bacon	eggs and bacon	(le) jambon = ham	
13) (le) fromage	cheese		
14) (les) légumes	vegetables	(les) petits pois = peas, (le) chou = cabbage, (les) haricots verts = string/ runner beans, (les) asperges = asparagus, (les) épinards = spinach, (les) spaghetti = spaghetti	

Leçon 13/Lesson 13

> to form the adverb, you generally add MENT to the feminine of the adjective:
>
> **sérieux** (serious) → **sérieuse** → **sérieusement**
> **rapide** (fast) → **rapide** → **rapidement**
> **immédiat** (immediate) → **immédiate** → **immédiatement**

careful! — exceptions: vite → vite; vrai → vraiment; mauvais → mal;
bon → bien

give the adverb:

> example: triste → tristement

seule	vite	drôle
bon	facile	stupide
rare	malheureux	simple
doux	lent	mauvais
heureux	vrai	général
dur	difficile	dangereux
profond	bête	certain

```
QUE = THAT

Je pense que tu es drôle.        =   I think (that) you're funny.
Je pense qu'il est drôle.        =   I think (that) he's funny.
```

translate:

a 1) Il espère qu'il a raison
   2) Je pense que tu as de la chance.
   3) Je sais qu'il a besoin d'argent.
   4) J'ai l'impression que tu es triste.

b 1) Do you know that he has a new car?
   2) Don't tell your mother that I'm hungry.
   3) I'm not sure that the store is open.
   4) We hope this mistake is the only one.

```
┌─────────────────────────────────────────────────────────────────────┐
│                                                                       │
│  CE QUE = WHAT                                                        │
│                                                                       │
│  EST-CE QUE C'EST CE QUE      =   Is that what you like?             │
│  VOUS AIMEZ?                                                          │
│                                                                       │
│  Oui, c'est ce que j'aime      ≠   Non, ce n'est pas ce que j'aime   │
│  Yes, that's what I like           No, that's not what I like         │
│                                                                       │
└─────────────────────────────────────────────────────────────────────┘
```

careful! — don't forget: What? = Quoi? Comment?

translate:

a 1) Elle veut ce que j'ai.
   2) Ce n'est pas ce que je mange d'habitude.
   3) Je sais ce que tu veux.
   4) Mange ce que tu peux.

b 1) Do you understand what she's saying?
   2) That's not what I want.
   3) Do you know what your grandfather thinks?
   4) His grandchildren say that he's very old.

CONTRAIRES/OPPOSITES — List 4

1) **La rivière est <u>profonde</u>**   ≠   **peu profonde**
   (The river is deep)   (shallow)

2) **Ce que tu dis est <u>vrai</u>**   ≠   **faux**
   (What you're saying's true)   (false)

3) **Le rubis est <u>vrai</u>**   ≠   **faux**
   (The ruby's real)   (fake)

4) **Tu es très <u>grossier</u>!**   ≠   **poli**
   (You're very rude)   (polite)

5) **La maison est <u>en pagaille</u>**   ≠   **rangée**
   (The house's a mess)   (tidy)

6) **Je suis <u>pour</u>**   ≠   **contre**
   (I'm for)   (against)

7) **Tu n'es pas <u>juste</u>**   ≠   **injuste**
   (You aren't fair)   (unfair)

8) **Mon parapluie n'est pas <u>sec</u>**   ≠   **mouillé**
   (My umbrella isn't dry)   (wet)

9) **L'enfant est <u>sage</u>**   ≠   **vilain**
   (The child's good)   (naughty)

translate:

a   1) Sa fille n'est pas souvent sage.
    2) Est-ce que mon pull est sec?
    3) La chambre est en pagaille.
    4) Est-ce que tu penses qu'ils sont frères?
    5) Il n'a pas raison.
    6) Elle pense que ses gosses sont vilains.

b   1) Is this thing real? Of course not!
    2) My stepfather is often unfair.
    3) You have a naughty brother.
    4) She feels like an ice cream. I'm all for it.
    5) My father's always very polite.
    6) Your room's a mess today.

REVISION OF OPPOSITES

(list 1 — page 9, list 2 — page 18, list 3 — page 42, list 4 — page 82)

translate and give opposites:

1) poor = **pauvre** ≠ **riche**
2) ugly = . . . ≠ . . .
3) young = . . . ≠ . . .
4) fat = . . . ≠ . . .
5) boring = . . . ≠ . . .
6) here = . . . ≠ . . .
7) weak = . . . ≠ . . .
8) quick = . . . ≠ . . .
9) hard = . . . ≠ . . .
10) after = . . . ≠ . . .
11) bad = . . . ≠ . . .
12) nice = . . . ≠ . . .
13) far = . . . ≠ . . .
14) short = . . . ≠ . . .
15) small = . . . ≠ . . .
16) dirty = . . . ≠ . . .
17) early = . . . ≠ . . .
18) cold = . . . ≠ . . .
19) naughty = . . . ≠ . . .
20) downstairs = . . . ≠ . . .
21) full = . . . ≠ . . .
22) high = . . . ≠ . . .
23) dangerous = . . . ≠ . . .
24) narrow = . . . ≠ . . .
25) heavy = . . . ≠ . . .
26) expensive = . . . ≠ . . .
27) first = . . . ≠ . . .
28) unfair = . . . ≠ . . .
29) deep = . . . ≠ . . .
30) polite = . . . ≠ . . .
31) dry = . . . ≠ . . .
32) against = . . . ≠ . . .
33) false = . . . ≠ . . .
34) a mess = . . . ≠ . . .
35) real = . . . ≠ . . .
36) thick = . . . ≠ . . .
37) new = . . . ≠ . . .
38) sweet = . . . ≠ . . .

VOCABULAIRE/VOCABULARY

	translation	synonym/ associated	opposite/ associated
1) **Qu'est-ce que vous désirez?**	What would you care for?		j'ai envie de = I feel like
2) **(la) belle-mère**	step-mother		(le) beau-père = step-father
3) **/(la) nièce /(la) tante**	/niece/aunt		(le) neveu = nephew, (l') oncle
4) **(le) grandpère**	grandfather	(les) grandsparents = grandparents	(la) grandmère = grandmother
5) **(la) petite-fille**	granddaughter	(le) petit-enfant = grand-child	(le) petit-fils = grandson
6) **(le) mari**	husband		(la) femme = wife
7) **(la) fille**	daughter		(le) fils = son
8) **par exemple**	for instance		
9) **j'aimerais**	I'd rather		
10) **(la) chose**	thing	(le) truc = gadget	
11) **étrange**	strange	curieux = odd, bizarre = bizarre	
12) **/pour (vous) /pendant (10 jours)**	/for (you) /for (10 days)	pendant, durant = during	
13) **heureusement**	happily	par bonheur = luckily, par hasard = by chance	malheureusement = unhappily, par malheur = unluckily
14) **Bien sûr que non!**	Of course not!		bien sûr = of course, certainement = certainly, absolument = absolutely

Leçon 14/Lesson 14

DIRECT OBJECT PRONOUNS

subject		object
je I	→	**me** me
tu you	→	**te** you
il he	→	**le** him, it
elle she	→	**la** her, it
nous we	→	**nous** us
vous you	→	**vous** you
ils/elles they	→	**les** them

careful! — me, te, le, la become m', t', l' in front of a vowel: je l'attends = I'm waiting for him/her

---

EST-CE QUE VOUS LA CONNAISSEZ?
Do you know her?

Oui, je la connais	=	Yes, I know her
Non, je ne la connais pas	=	No, I don't know her.

---

je m'entends ≠ **je ne m'entends pas**	I hear me ≠ I don't hear me
je t'entends ≠ **je ne t'entends pas**	I hear you ≠ I don't hear you
je l'entends ≠ **je ne l'entends pas**	I hear him/her/it ≠ I don't hear him/her/it
je nous entends ≠ **je ne nous entends pas**	I hear us ≠ I don't hear us
je vous entends ≠ **je ne vous entends pas**	I hear you ≠ I don't hear you
je les entends ≠ **je ne les entends pas**	I hear them ≠ I don't hear them

translate:

a 1) Je la connais bien.
   2) Elle ne l'a plus.
   3) Je ne vous entends pas.
   4) Je le vois souvent.

b 1) Do you see me?
   2) Write it quickly!
   3) Don't drink it!
   4) I don't believe you.

translate:

a   1) Il y a beaucoup de meubles dans l'appartement.
    2) Ta cuisine n'est pas jolie.
    3) La salle de bains est sale.
    4) Les rideaux sont trop longs.
    5) Ta chambre à coucher est trop petite.
    6) Est-ce que tu as besoin d'aller aux toilettes?

b   1) The elevator/lift doesn't work.
    2) Write me a letter soon.
    3) The closet (cupboard) is very high.
    4) Do you need stamps?
    5) Our dining room is very big.
    6) My bed is in the living room.

VOCABULAIRE/VOCABULARY

	translation	synonym/ associated	opposite/ associated
1) (la) chambre à coucher	bedroom	(le) lit = bed	
2) (la) pièce	room	ma chambre = my room; (la) salle de séjour, (le) salon = living room; la salle à manger = dining-room, (la) cuisine = kitchen	
3) (la) casserole	pot	(la) poêle = pan	
4) (la) salle de bain	bathroom	(les) toilettes = toilet, (le) petit coin = the John, (l')évier = kitchen sink	
5) (le) tapis	rug	(la) moquette = carpet	
6) (le) rideau	curtain		
7) (la) lampe	lamp	(l')ampoule = bulb	
8) Vous trouvez?	Do you think so?		
9) Cela ne marche pas!	It doesn't work!		
10) (les) meubles	furniture	(le) divan), (le) canapé = couch, (le) sofa = sofa	
11) (l')ascenseur	lift, elevator		
12) (l')étage	floor	par terre = on the floor	
13) (le) placard	cupboard, closet	(l')étagère = shelf	
14) (la) lettre	letter	(le) timbre = stamp, (l')enveloppe = envelope, (la) carte postale = postcard	

Leçon 14/Lesson 14 appendix

INDIRECT OBJECT PRONOUNS

subject		object
je I	→	**me (moi)** (to) me
tu you	→	**te (toi)** (to) you
il he, it	→	**lui** (to) him, it
elle she, it	→	**lui (elle)** (to) her, it
nous we	→	**nous** (to) us
vous you	→	**vous** (to) you
ils/elles they	→	**leur (eux, elles)** (to) them

careful! — this is a real difficulty since these indirect pronouns are
non-existent in English. They are generally used when 'to' is said
or implied: je lui écris = I'm writing to him.
— after prepositions: avec moi = with me, pour eux, pour elles = for
them
— after commands: dites-moi = tell me, écris-moi = write to me
— c'est moi = it's me

Est-ce que vous <u>leur</u> écrivez quelquefois?
Do you sometimes write to them?

Oui, je <u>leur</u> écris quelquefois.	=	Yes, I sometimes write to them.
Non, je ne <u>leur</u> écris jamais.	=	No, I never write to them.

je m'écris ≠ je ne m'écris pas	I'm writing to me ≠ I'm not writing to me
je t'écris ≠ je ne t'écris pas	I'm writing to you ≠ I'm not writing to you
je lui écris ≠ je ne lui écris pas	I'm writing to him/her ≠ I'm not writing to him/her
je nous écris ≠ je ne nous écris pas	I'm writing to us ≠ I'm not writing to us
je vous écris ≠ je ne vous écris pas	I'm writing to you ≠ I'm not writing to you
je leur écris ≠ je ne leur écris pas	I'm writing to them ≠ I'm not writing to them

translate:

1) Please, send me a cake.
2) I can show her the book tonight.
3) Tell me the truth.
4) Don't answer them.
5) Write me a letter every day.
6) I'm talking to you.

VERBS FOLLOWED BY À

donner à	=	to give to
elle leur donne un livre		she gives them a book
appartenir à	=	to belong to
la maison lui appartient		the house belongs to him/her
écrire à	=	to write to
Ils nous écrivent		they write to us
expliquer à	=	to explain to
explique-moi la leçon		explain the lesson to me
penser à	=	to think of
je pense à toi		I think of you
dire à	=	to say to/to tell
je vais leur dire ce que je pense		I'm going to tell them what I think
je ne comprends pas ce qu'elle		I don't understand what she's
lui dit		saying to him

translate:

1) Pensez-vous souvent à moi?
2) Elle me dit toujours tout.
3) Ce chien ne leur appartient pas.
4) Mes parents ne lui parlent pas.
5) Écris-moi ce que tu penses.
6) Donne-lui ton vélo.

Leçon 15/Lesson 15

FUTURE

je travaill**erai** ≠ je ne travaill**erai** pas	I'll work ≠ I won't work	
tu travaill**eras** ≠ tu ne travaill**erais** pas	you'll work ≠ you won't work	

il
elle } travaill**era** ≠ elle } ne travaill**era**
on   on)   pas

he
she'll } work ≠ she } won't work
one)   one)

nous travaill**erons** ≠ nous ne
                    travaill**erons** pas

we'll work ≠ we won't work

vous travaill**erez** ≠ vous ne
                    travaill**erez** pas

you'll work ≠ you won't work

ils
elles } travaill**eront** ≠ ils } ne
                    elles)
                    travaill**eront** pas

they'll work ≠ they won't work

No difficulty with this tense! Simply add the underlined endings to the infinitive of all groups, except for that ending in RE, where you drop the 'e' (croire → je croirai), and remember a few exceptions.

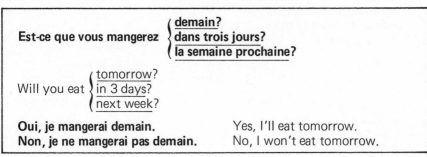

Est-ce que vous mangerez { **demain?**
                                { **dans trois jours?**
                                { **la semaine prochaine?**

Will you eat { tomorrow?
             { in 3 days?
             { next week?

Oui, je mangerai demain.   Yes, I'll eat tomorrow.
Non, je ne mangerai pas demain.   No, I won't eat tomorrow.

careful! — use the future after 'quand' (nous mangerons quand ils arriveront = we'll eat when they come)

give French affirmative and negative answers:

> example: Shall/will we go to the restaurant tonight?
> Oui, nous irons au restaurant ce soir.
> Non, nous n'irons pas au restaurant ce soir.

a 1) Will you come tomorrow?
  2) Will they take the plane to Chicago?
  3) Will you tell him why he's wrong?
  4) Will he be hungry when he leaves?
  5) Will she go to England next week?
  6) Shall/will we go shopping next Saturday?
  7) Will you be able to help me tomorrow?
  8) Will you go to bed in an hour?

translate only:

b 1) I'll try to see him next week.
  2) He'll eat with me tomorrow.
  3) We'll study together this weekend.
  4) She'll make us a big cake tonight.
  5) My father will go to London in a week.
  6) They'll have to speak with the teacher soon.
  7) I'll play with you before dinner.
  8) Will you go to bed after me?

SOME IRREGULAR VERBS IN THE FUTURE

1) **ACHETER** = j'achèterai
   (to buy)

2) **ALLER** = j'irai
   (to go)

3) **APPELER** = j'appellerai
   (to call)

4) **S'ASSEOIR** = je m'assoirai
   (to sit)

5) **BOIRE** = je boirai
   (to drink)

6) **CHOISIR** = je choisirai
   (to choose)

7) **COMMENCER** = je commencerai
   (to begin)

8) **COMPRENDRE** = je comprendrai
   (to understand)

9) **CONNAÎTRE** = je connaitrai
   (to know)

10) **COURIR** = je courrai
    (to run)

11) **DEVENIR** = je deviendrai
    (to become)

12) **DIRE** = je dirai
    (to say)

13) **ÉCRIRE** = j'écrirai
    (to write)

14) **ENTENDRE** = j'entendrai
    (to hear)

15) **ENVOYER** = j'enverrai
    (to send)

16) **ESPÉRER** = j'espérerai
    (to hope)

17) **FAIRE** = je ferai
    (to do/to make)

18) **JETER** = je jetterai
    (to throw)

19) **LIRE** = je lirai
    (to read)

20) **MANGER** = je mangerai
    (to eat)

21) **METTRE** = je mettrai
    (to put)

22) **OUVRIR** = j'ouvrirai
    (to open)

23) **PARTIR** = je partirai
    (to leave)

24) **POUVOIR** = je pourrai
    (can)

25) **PRENDRE** = je prendrai
    (to take)

26) **RECEVOIR** = je recevrai
    (to receive)

27) **REPONDRE** = je répondrai
    (to answer)

28) **RIRE** = je rirai
    (to laugh)

29) **SAVOIR** = je saurai
    (to know)

30) **SENTIR** = je sentirai
    (to feel)

31) **SORTIR** = je sortirai
    (to go out)

32) **VENDRE** = je vendrai
    (to sell)

33) **VENIR** = je viendrai
    (to come)

34) **VIVRE** = je vivrai
    (to live)

35) **VOIR** = je verrai
    (to see)

36) **VOULOIR** = je voudrai
    (to want)

translate:

a   1) Qu'est-ce que tu feras demain?
    2) Elle dira non.
    3) Nous jouerons au tennis ensemble dans une semaine.
    4) Je le ferai la semaine prochaine.
    5) Nous verrons nos grands-parents demain.
    6) Je boirai beaucoup de lait ce soir.
    7) Elle ne sortira pas de l'hôpital avant Noël.
    8) Je n'ouvrirai pas la porte.

b   1) I'll take my vacation next month.
    2) I'll be able to see you in a week.
    3) What will you do tomorrow?
    4) My parents will buy a new boat next week.
    5) They'll call him in a week.
    6) We'll begin the work next year.
    7) They'll put the pool in front of the house.
    8) We'll sit on the sofa.

VOCABULAIRE/VOCABULARY

	translation	synonym/ associated	opposite/ associated
1) (le) hobby	hobby	(le) violon d'Ingres, (le) passe-temps = pastime	
2) (le) sport	sport	(le) football = (Association) football, (le) football américain = American football, (le) volley-ball = volleyball, (le) base-ball = baseball	
3) /Noël/Pâques	/Christmas/Easter		
4) rester	to stay		partir = to leave
5) (les) vacances	vacation	en vacances = on vacation	
6) (la) plage	beach	(le) sable = sand, (la) planche à voile = windsurfer, sailboard	(la) piscine = pool
7) nager	to swim	faire la planche = to float, aller se baigner = to go swimming	se noyer = to drown
8) patiner	to skate	faire du patin à glace = to iceskate, faire du patin à roulettes = to roller-skate, patins(m) = skates	
9) jouer au tennis	to play tennis		
10) (le) jour ferié	holiday		
11) skier	to ski	faire du ski = to go skiing	
12) dire	to say	raconter = to tell	
13) faire	to do, to make		
14) (l')hôtel	hotel	(l')auberge = inn, (la) chambre = room, bonne, (la) femme de chambre = maid	

Leçon 16/Lesson 16

SI = IF

present   future

Si j'ai le temps,   **je vous aiderai.**
If I have time,   I'll help you.

Si vous avez le temps, est-ce que vous m'aiderez?
If you have the time, will you help me?

Oui, si j'ai le temps, je vous aiderai.
Yes, if I have time, I'll help you.

Non, si j'ai le temps, je ne vous aiderai pas.
No, if I have time, I won't help you.

no problem! — the structure is the same in French and in English

translate:

1) If I bring you a cake, will you eat it?
2) If she breaks a plate, will you pay for it?
3) If we have a lot of money, (shall) will we go shopping?
4) If she's hungry, she'll eat lunch.
5) If you're thirsty, I'll give you a glass of milk.
6) If you're very hot, will you go swimming?
7) If she can't do her homework alone, will you help her?
8) If the zoo's dirty, the animals will be sick.
9) If the bed's comfortable, she'll sleep on it.
10) If you get a new animal, will you show it to me?
11) If we go to the mountains, we'll go skiing.
12) If they go on vacation, will it be at Christmas?
13) If he isn't well, he'll stay in bed.
14) If she isn't ill any more, we'll play tennis tomorrow.

translate and put in the French negative:

example: Si le vin est bon, je le boirai.
If the wine is good, I'll drink it.
Si le vin n'est pas bon, je ne le boirai pas.

1) Si le repas est froid, je serai très contente.
2) Si l'oiseau est malade, je serai triste.
3) Si la plage est sale, j'irai dans la forêt.
4) Si tu te casses la jambe, est-ce que tu resteras au lit?
5) Si tout le monde a faim, nous mangerons tôt.
6) Si tu viens nous sortirons.
7) Qu'est-ce que tu feras si je suis malade?
8) Est-ce que nous irons en vacances si nous avons beaucoup d'argent?
9) S'il pleut, est-ce que nous irons à la plage?
10) Si mon ami préféré y va, j'irai aussi.
11) Si nous allons au zoo cet après-midi, nous verrons des singes, des ours et des serpents.
12) Si tu as à aller chez le médecin, est-ce que tu prendras le train?
13) Même si tu penses qu'il est bête, ne dis rien.
14) Si tu me montres tes devoirs, je te montrerai les miens.

VOCABULAIRE/VOCABULARY

	translation	synonym/ associated	opposite/ associated
1) même	even		
2) (l')animal	animal	(la) queue = tail, (l')ours = bear, (le) lion = lion, (le) tigre = tiger, (le) serpent = snake, (l')éléphant = elephant, (le) singe = monkey, (le) zoo = zoo	
3) apporter	ιo bring		
4) casser	to break		
5) (la) rue	street	(la) route = road	
6) confortable	comfortable		inconfortable = uncomfortable
7) (l')animal domestique	pet		
8) (l')oiseau	bird	(le) canard = duck	
9) montrer	to show		
10) malade	sick, ill		bien = well
11) (la) montagne	mountain		(la) vallée = valley
12) favori	favourite	préféré	
13) (la) forêt	forest	(l')arbre = tree	
14) drôle	funny	amusant = amusing	

Leçon 17/Lesson 17

---

translate and put in the French negative:

example: Do you ever put water in your wine?

Est-ce qu'il vous arrive de mettre de l'eau dans votre vin?
Non, je ne mets jamais d'eau dans mon vin.

a   1)   Does your neighbour ever go on vacation?
2)   Do you ever eat lemons?
3)   Does she ever take a bath in the evening?
4)   Do they ever buy flowers?

b   1)   Le jardinier de mes parents ne boit jamais de bière.
2)   Est-ce qu'il arrive à ta mère de boire du café?
3)   Est-ce qu'il t'arrive d'être en retard?
4)   Je ne mets jamais de sel sur les pommes.

THE FRENCH LIVE IN THE PRESENT!!!

REGARDER = to watch, pay attention to

je regarde la télévision maintenant	I'm watching television now
je regarde souvent la télévision	I often watch television
je regarde la télévision depuis une demi-heure **(Cela fait une demi-heure que je regarde la télévision)**	I've been watching television for half an hour

careful! — you must get used to the multiple use of the French present . . .

Elle est divorcée depuis trois ans.	She's been divorced for three years.
Je travaille ici depuis Pâques.	I've been working here since Easter.
Nous habitons ici depuis six mois.	We've lived here for the last six months.
Depuis quand êtes-vous mariés?	How long have you been married?

translate:

1) Je mange depuis quinze minutes.
2) Nous sommes mariés depuis février.
3) Elle parle depuis une heure.
4) Les enfants dorment maintenant.
5) Les enfants dorment beaucoup.
6) Les enfants dorment depuis une demi-heure.

JE VAIS . . .	I'M GOING TO . . .
Je vais bientôt rentrer.	I'm going to go home soon.
Il va lui parler demain.	He's going to talk to her tomorrow.
Nous allons acheter une nouvelle voiture.	We're going to buy a new car.

translate:

a 1) Est-ce que tu vas aller à la plage cet après-midi.
   2) Nous allons manger des fruits ce soir.
   3) Je vais prendre un bain à neuf heures.
   4) Il ne va pas mettre de sucre dans son lait.

b 1) Are you going to come tonight?
   2) She's going to take the elevator/lift.
   3) Are they going to buy this strange thing?
   4) I hope you're going to help us.

translate:

a 1) Le professeur parle depuis une heure.
   2) Je suis ici depuis janvier.
   3) Est-ce qu'il arrive aux enfants de boire du vin?
   4) Je vais à la ferme et je vais acheter du lait.
   5) Depuis quand est-ce que tu vas à l'école?
   6) Nous allons écrire des lettres ce soir.

b 1) I've known him for ten years.
   2) My parents never drink wine.
   3) We've been living in New York for eight months.
   4) She's eating now. She always eats at eight o'clock.
   5) Do you ever take a shower in the morning?
   6) You've been talking for an hour. You always talk too much.

VOCABULAIRE/VOCABULARY

	translation	synonym/ associated	opposite associated
1) (un) pays	(a) country	(la) campagne = the country	
2) (le) voisin	neighbour		
3) (le) fermier	farmer	(la) ferme = farm	
4) /(le) cheval/(la) chèvre/(la) vache/(le) cochon	/horse/goat/cow/pig		
5) (la) terre	land		
6) (le) prochain	(the) next	(le) suivant = (the) following	
7) (les) fruits	fruit	(la) pomme = apple, (la) poire = pear, (l')orange = orange, (le) citron = lemon, (le) pamplemousse = grapefruit, (la) banane = banana, (la) cerise = cherry, (la) fraise = strawberry	
8) (le) bain	bath	prendre un bain = to take a bath, (la) douche = shower	
9) (le) café	coffee	(le) thé = tea	
10) (le) début	beginning, start	(le) commencement	(la) fin = end
11) /(le) sel/(le) sucre	/salt/sugar		(le) poivre = pepper, (la) moutarde = mustard
12) /brun/vert/gris /jaune	/brown/green/grey /yellow	marron = chestnut	
13) (la) fleur	flower	(le) jardin = garden, (le) jardinier = gardener, (l')herbe = grass, (la) plante = plant	
14) (le) vin	wine	(la) bière = beer	

93

Leçon 18/Lesson 18

DU, DE LA, DES = SOME, ANY

{ je mange <u>du</u> pain =
{ je ne mange pas <u>de</u> pain

{ I eat (some) bread =
{ I don't eat (any) bread

{ je mange <u>de la</u> viande =
{ je ne mange pas <u>de</u> viande

{ I eat (some) meat =
{ I don't eat (any) meat

{ je mange <u>de l'</u>omelette =
{ je ne mange pas <u>d'</u>omelette

{ I eat (some) omelette =
{ I don't eat (any) omelette

{ je mange <u>des</u> pommes =
{ je ne mange pas <u>de</u> pommes

{ I eat (some) apples =
{ I don't eat (any) apples

---

careful! —'some' and 'any' are optional in English, but the articles are
      obligatory in French.
      don't forget: **d'** or **de** after a negative verb

translate:

a   1)   Je bois de l'eau.
      2)   Elle mange rarement du sucre.
      3)   Est-ce qu'elle a du chocolat?
      4)   Nous n'avons pas de romans à lire cet été.

b   1)   I want some money at once.
      2)   I never drink any coffee.
      3)   Will you need some help?
      4)   I don't have any furniture in my room.

```
EN = SOME/ANY

Avez-vous du temps?                    Have you (some) time?

Oui, j'en ai.                          Yes, I have (some).
Non, je n'en ai pas.                   No, I don't have any.
```

careful! — 'en' as a pronoun is often used in French

```
Voulez-vous du lait?        =   Do you want (some) milk?

Oui, j'en veux.             =   Yes, I want some.
Non, je n'en veux pas.      =   No, I don't want any.
```

translate:

a 1) Je n'en veux pas.
   2) Est-ce que tu en as?
   3) Je n'en mange jamais.
   4) Est-ce que vous en voulez?

b 1) Does she want any?
   2) I feel like chocolate, but I don't have any.
   3) Why don't you buy some?
   4) Are you sure you don't need any?

QUELQUES = A FEW, SOME

J'ai **quelques problèmes**

I have $\begin{cases} \text{a few} \\ \text{some} \end{cases}$ problems

---

UN PEU DE = A LITTLE, SOME

J'ai **un peu de temps**

I have $\begin{cases} \text{some} \\ \text{a little} \end{cases}$ time.

Du temps? — J'**en ai un peu**

Time? — I have $\begin{cases} \text{some} \\ \text{a little} \end{cases}$

---

careful! —use 'un peu de' for things which cannot be counted (money, water, time, etc) and 'quelques' for things which can be counted (apples, cars, persons)

translate:

a   1) Nous avons quelques bons copains.
     2) Elle a un peu d'argent dans son sac.
     3) Est-ce que tu as besoin de quelques livres pour les vacances?
     4) Il y a un peu de lait dans le frigidaire.

b   1) I only have a little money.
     2) France has only a few good actresses.
     3) The story has only a few pages.
     4) England has very few airports.

ADVERBS, etc . . . — List 3

1)	**au lieu de**	instead of
2)	**de temps en temps**	from time to time
	de temps à autre	now and then, once in a while
3)	**cependant**	however
4)	**exactement**	exactly
5)	**pour**	to, in order to
	afin de	so as to
	pour que	so that
6)	**bien que, quoique**	although
7)	**malgré**	in spite of
8)	**entre-temps**	in the meantime, in the meanwhile
9)	**donc**	so, therefore, thus

translate:

a   1) Au lieu de dépenser ton argent, garde-le.
    2) Malgré la pluie, nous irons nous promener.
    3) Entre-temps nous mangerons.
    4) C'est trop cher, je ne peux pas l'acheter.
    5) L'histoire est intéressante, cependant le film est mauvais.
    6) Je suis à l'aéroport pour prendre l'avion.

b   1) We go to the United States from time to time.
    2) He works hard so as to help his parents.
    3) Speak slowly and I'll understand you.
    4) That's exactly what I want.
    5) He's very nice, however, I don't like him.
    6) We go to the restaurant now and then.

VOCABULAIRE/VOCABULARY

	translation	synonym/ associated	opposite/ associated
1) (l')aéroport	airport	(le) pilote = pilot	
2) /(les) États-Unis /(l')Angleterre /(la) France	/the United States /England /France	(les) Français = (the) French	(le) français = (the) French (language)
3) se reposer	to rest		
4) (le) genre	kind	(la) sorte = sort	
5) (l')histoire	story	(le) roman = novel	
6) (l')acteur	actor		(l')actrice = actress
7) (l')artiste	artist	(le) peintre	
8) croire	to believe		
9) meilleur	better	the best = (le) mieux, (le) meilleur	pire = worse
10) (l')anniversaire	birthday		
11) fermé	closed		ouvert = open
12) dépenser	to spend		
13) (le) prix	price		
14) (le) morceau	piece		

Leçon 19/Lesson 19

riche	=	rich
plus riche (que)	=	richer (than)
le, la (les) plus riche (s)	=	the richest

Est-ce que ton frère est plus riche que toi?	=	Is your brother <u>richer than</u> you are?
Oui, mon frère est plus riche que moi.	=	Yes, my brother is <u>richer than</u> I am.
Non, mon frère n'est pas plus riche que moi.	=	No, my brother isn't <u>richer than</u> I am.
Non, mon frère est moins riche que moi.	=	No, my brother is <u>less rich than</u> I am.

premier = first
second, deuxième = second
troisième = third
quatrième = fourth
cinquième = fifth

translate:

a 1) Je suis plus grande que ma mère.
  2) Son vélo est plus cher que le tien.
  3) Je le trouve plus drôle que d'habitude.
  4) C'est le plus grand de la classe.
  5) Il perd plus d'argent que moi.
  6) Je l'aime plus que sa sœur.

b 1) Your dog's uglier than mine.
  2) She's the prettiest in the family.
  3) He's the richest man in the country.
  4) You're the most stupid person here.
  5) She's nicer than her teacher.
  6) The book's more interesting than the movie.

AUSSI . . . QUE	=	AS . . . AS
Il est <u>aussi</u> riche <u>que</u> moi.	=	He's as rich as me.
Il n'est <u>pas aussi</u> riche <u>que</u> moi.	=	He's not as/so rich as me.

IRREGULAR ADJECTIVES

bon (good)	**mauvais** (bad)	**peu** (little)	**beaucoup** (much)
↓	↓	↓	↓
meilleur (better)	**pire** (worse)	**moins** (less)	**plus** (more)
↓	↓	↓	↓
le mieux (best)	**le pire** (worst)	**le moins** (least)	**le plus** (most)

translate:

a 1) Cette voiture est plus chère que l'autre.
   2) Est-ce que c'est le restaurant le moins cher que tu connais?
   3) Elle ne croit pas que sa grand-mère est moins intelligente que son grand-père.
   4) J'ai plus d'argent que vous.
   5) Il est pire que son frère.
   6) Je trouve que cet acteur est meilleur que les autres.

b 1) Who is the most interesting teacher in your school?
   2) I think that this is the best movie this year.
   3) You're the worst person.
   4) She isn't as beautiful as her sister.
   5) France is almost as big as Germany.
   6) This actor isn't as good as his brother.

1)	**comme** **puisque**	since
2)	**immédiatement,** **tout de suite**	immediately, at once
3)	**si,** **tellement**	so
4)	**plus tard** **≠ plus tôt**	later ≠ earlier
5)	**à cause de**	because of
6)	**surtout**	especially, above all
7)	**(juste) au cas où**	(just) in case
8)	**récemment,** **il n'y a pas longtemps**	recently, not long ago
9)	**dès que**	as soon as
10)	**exprès** **intentionnellement**	on purpose intentionally
11)	**puis** **ensuite**	then
12)	**une fois** **≠ deux fois**	once ≠ twice

translate:

a   1) Puisque tu ne peux pas venir, je viendrai.
     2) Je suis contente parce que tu es là.
     3) Fais-le tout de suite.
     4) Surtout n'oublie pas mon anniversaire.
     5) Je ne l'ai pas fait exprès.
     6) Je veux gagner une fois.

b   1) Since you're here let's start breakfast.
     2) Because of the rain, we'll stay at home.
     3) As soon as he writes to you, tell me.
     4) Since it rains, take an umbrella.
     5) I'll buy it later.
     6) I like her family, especially her mother.

VOCABULAIRE/VOCABULARY

	translation	synonym/ associated	opposite associated
1) aimer	to love	aimer bien = to like	détester = to hate = haïr
2) pousser	to push		tirer = to pull
3) rire	to laugh		pleurer = to cry
4) ne pas prêter attention à	to ignore		faire attention à = to pay attention to
5) trouver	to find		perdre = to lose
6) échouer	to fail		réussir = to succeed
7) acheter	to buy		vendre = to sell
8) gagner	to win		perdre = to lose
9) mettre (manteau)	to put on (coat)	porter = to wear	enlever = to take off
10) être d'accord (avec)	to agree (with)		ne pas être d'accord = to disagree
11) démarrer	to start	commencer	arrêter = to stop, cesser, arrêter = to quit
12) allumer	to turn on, to put on		éteindre = to turn off, to put off
13) s'endormir	to fall asleep		se réveiller = to wake up, se lever = to get up
14) fermer	to close, to shut		ouvrir = to open

106

Leçon 20/Lesson 20

TOUJOURS/ENCORE = STILL

Est-ce que tu es $\begin{cases} \textbf{encore} \\ \textbf{toujours} \end{cases}$ ici? = Oui, je suis $\begin{cases} \textbf{encore} \\ \textbf{toujours} \end{cases}$ ici.

Are you still here?　　　　　　　Yes, I'm still here.

careful! — 'toujours' can also be translated by 'always'

NE . . . PLUS = NOT . . . ANY MORE (not . . . any longer)

Non, je ne suis plus ici.　　　= No, I'm not here any more (any longer).

---

translate:

a　1) Elle se souvient encore de lui.
　　2) Je n'habite plus l'Angleterre.
　　3) Nous ne voulons plus partir.
　　4) Elle ne sait pas encore s'habiller toute seule.

b　1) She's still afraid of her father.
　　2) Are they still in London?
　　3) He doesn't smoke any more.
　　4) I don't want to go to school any more.

> **CES** = THESE
> **CES . . . LÀ** = THOSE
>
> **Je veux <u>ces</u> livres et <u>ces</u> stylos-<u>là</u>.** =   I want <u>these</u> books and <u>those</u> pens.

translate:

1) Ces manteaux sont mouillés et ces parapluies-là sont secs.
2) Ces chaussures sont les miennes. Est-ce que ces bottes-là sont les tiennes?
3) Ces chiens ne sont pas à elle, mais ces chats-là sont les siens.
4) Ces gens-là ne sont pas très gentils.

> **WHAT**
>
> | | | |
> |---|---|---|
> | **<u>Quoi</u>?** | = | <u>What</u>? |
> | **<u>Qu'est-ce que</u> c'est** | = | <u>What</u> is it? |
> | **Je sais <u>ce que</u> tu veux.** | = | I know <u>what</u> you want. |

TO KNOW =

SAVOIR
(something, facts, etc.)

CONNAÎTRE
(persons, places, etc.)

Est-ce que vous

<u>savez</u> $\begin{cases} \text{çà?} \\ \text{conduire?} \\ \text{la réponse?} \end{cases}$

Est-ce que vous

<u>connaissez</u> $\begin{cases} \text{cette femme?} \\ \text{New York?} \\ \text{cette maison?} \end{cases}$

Do you <u>know</u> $\begin{cases} \text{that?} \\ \text{how to drive?} \\ \text{the answer?} \end{cases}$

Do you <u>know</u> $\begin{cases} \text{this woman?} \\ \text{New York?} \\ \text{this house?} \end{cases}$

careful! — 'je <u>sais</u> conduire' = 'I <u>know how to</u> drive'

translate:

a   1) Je ne connais pas ce film-là.
    2) Je ne sais pas parler français.
    3) Est-ce que tu connais mon frère?
    4) Je ne sais plus ma leçon.
    5) Je ne connais pas Londres.
    6) Est-ce que tu sais s'il viendra?

b   1) He doesn't know the answer.
    2) I don't know that store.
    3) My mother knows how to drive.
    4) She does not know Peter.
    5) She doesn't know I'm coming.
    6) He doesn't know this book.

	translation	synonym/ associated	opposite/ associated
1) se lever	to stand up		s'asseoir = to sit down
2) être debout	to be standing		être assis = to be sitting
3) s'habiller	to get dressed		se déshabiller = to get undressed
4) donner	to give		prendre = to take
5) envoyer	to send		recevoir = to get, to receive
6) se dépêcher	to hurry up	se presser = to rush	prendre son temps = to take one's time
7) partir	to leave		rester = to stay, to remain
8) enseigner	to teach		apprendre = to learn
9) revenir	to come back		s'en aller = to go away
10) jeter	to throw		attraper = to catch
11) laisser	to let		interdire = to forbid
12) se marier	to get married		divorcer = to get divorced
13) mourir	to die		naître = to be born
14) oublier	to forget		se souvenir = to remember

Leçon 21/Lesson 21

PASSÉ COMPOSÉ = PAST TENSE

J'ai travaillé $\begin{cases} \text{hier} \\ \text{l'année dernière} \\ \text{il y a quatre jours} \end{cases}$ = I worked $\begin{cases} \text{yesterday} \\ \text{last year} \\ \text{four days ago} \end{cases}$

careful! — form the past tense with the present of 'avoir' plus the past participle of the verb.

j'ai travaillé	≠ je n'ai pas travaillé
tu as travaillé	tu n'as pas travaillé
il elle } a travaillé on	il elle } n'a pas travaillé on
nous avons travaillé	nous n'avons pas travaillé
vous avez travaillé	vous n'avez pas travaillé
ils elles } ont travaillé	ils elles } n'ont pas travaillé

> **Est-ce que vous avez regardé la télévision hier?**
> Did you watch television yesterday?
>
> **Oui, j'ai regardé la télévision hier.**
> Yes, I watched television yesterday.
>
> **Non, je n'ai pas regardé la télévision hier.**
> No, I didn't watch television yesterday.

PAST PARTICIPLE

parler	→	**parlé**
finir	→	**fini**
vendre	→	**vendu**

---

translate:

a 1) Ils ont arrêté de travailler à six heures.
   2) Elle a payé dix dollars pour ce truc.
   3) Le garçon nous à donné l'addition il y a une heure.
   4) Je t'ai téléphoné hier soir.
   5) Tu as dormi dans le camion hier.
   6) L'école a fermé il y a deux jours et tout le monde est sur la plage.

b 1) Did you have to go to school during Easter?
   2) We gave our parents a beautiful art book.
   3) The waiter brought us French fries with the meat.
   4) He phoned me yesterday.
   5) I ate a grapefruit and a pear an hour ago.
   6) I heard my mother cry last week.

112

1) **ACHETER** = acheté
   (to buy)

2) **APPELER** = appelé
   (to call)

3) **APPORTER** = apporté
   (to bring)

4) **APPRENDRE** = appris
   (to learn)

5) **ARRÊTER** = arrêté
   (to stop)

6) **ATTENDRE** = attendu
   (to wait)

7) **ATTRAPER** = attrapé
   (to catch)

8) **AVOIR** = eu
   (to have)

9) **AVOIR BESOIN DE** = eu
   (to need)   **besoin de**

10) **BOIRE** = bu
    (to drink)

11) **CACHER** = caché
    (to hide)

12) **CASSER** = cassé
    (to break)

13) **CHOISIR** = choisi
    (to choose)

14) **COMMENCER** = commencé
    (to begin)

15) **COMPRENDRE** = compris
    (to understand)

16) **CONNAÎTRE** = connu
    (to know)

17) **CONTINUER** = continué
    (to continue)

18) **COUPER** = coupé
    (to cut)

19) **COURIR** = couru
    (to run)

20) **COUTER** = coûté
    (to cost)

21) **DÉCHIRER** = déchiré
    (to tear)

22) **DÉPENSER** = dépensé
    (to spend)

23) **DEVENIR** = devenu
    (to become)

24) **DEVOIR** = dû
    (to have to)

25) **DIRE** = dit
    (to say)

26) **DONNER** = donné
    (to give)

27) **DORMIR** = dormi
    (to sleep)

28) **ÉCRIRE** = écrit
    (to write)

29) **ENSEIGNER** = enseigné
    (to teach)

30) **ENTENDRE** = entendu
    (to hear)

31) **ENVOYER** = envoyé
    (to send)

32) **ESPÉRER** = espéré
    (to hope)

1) **ÊTRE** = <u>été</u>
   (to be)

2) **FAIRE** = <u>fait</u>
   (to make)

3) **FERMER** = fer<u>mé</u>
   (to close)

4) **FINIR** = fi<u>ni</u>
   (to finish)

5) **GARDER** = gar<u>dé</u>
   (to keep)

6) **JETER** = je<u>té</u>
   (to throw)

7) **LAISSER** = lais<u>sé</u>
   (to leave)

8) **LIRE** = <u>lu</u>
   (to read)

9) **MANGER** = man<u>gé</u>
   (to eat)

10) **METTRE** = m<u>is</u>
    (to put)

11) **OUVRIR** = ouv<u>ert</u>
    (to open)

12) **PARLER** = par<u>lé</u>
    (to speak)

13) **PAYER** = pa<u>yé</u>
    (to pay)

14) **PENSER** = pen<u>sé</u>
    (to think)

15) **PORTER** = por<u>té</u>
    (to carry)

16) **POUVOIR** = <u>pu</u>
    (to be able to)

17) **PRENDRE** = pr<u>is</u>
    (to take)

18) **PRETER** = prê<u>té</u>
    (to lend)

19) **RECEVOIR** = re<u>çu</u>
    (to get)

20) **RENCONTRER** = rencont<u>ré</u>
    (to meet)

21) **RÉPONDRE** = répon<u>du</u>
    (to answer)

22) **RIRE** = <u>ri</u>
    (to laugh)

23) **SAVOIR** = <u>su</u>
    (to know)

24) **SECOUER** = seco<u>ué</u>
    (to shake)

25) **SENTIR** = sen<u>ti</u>
    (to feel)

26) **SIGNIFIER** = signif<u>ié</u>
    (to mean)

27) **TROUVER** = trou<u>vé</u>
    (to find)

28) **VENDRE** = ven<u>du</u>
    (to sell)

29) **VIVRE** = <u>vécu</u>
    (to live)

30) **VOIR** = <u>vu</u>
    (to see)

31) **VOLER** = vo<u>lé</u>
    (to fly)

32) **VOULOIR** = voul<u>u</u>
    (to want)

translate and give negative answer:

> example: Did she love her husband?
> Est-ce qu'elle a aimé son mari?
> Non, elle n'a pas aimé son mari.

a 1) Did he spend a lot of money?
   2) Did you do it with your brother?
   3) Did you meet those nice people?
   4) Were you in England last week?
   5) Did they give her flowers?
   6) Did she buy a new coat last week?

translate and put in the French interrogative:

> example: J'ai acheté une nouvelle maison il y a un an.
> I bought a new house a year ago.
> Est-ce que tu as acheté une nouvelle maison il y a un an?

b 1) Nous avons caché le cadeau dans le placard.
   2) Je lui ai parlé hier.
   3) Elle a déchiré sa robe il y a une heure.
   4) Le professeur a arrêté d'enseigner l'année dernière.
   5) Vous avez dû partir tôt à cause de la neige.
   6) Tu as écrit à ta grand-mère l'été dernier.

translate and put in the interrogative and negative:

> example: I read this book very fast
> J'ai lu ce livre très vite
> Est-ce que tu as lu ce livre très vite?
> Non, je n'ai pas lu ce livre très vite

1) He needed some money last night.
2) He called me late yesterday.
3) He showed me his new pet last Sunday.
4) We gave her a gift for her birthday.
5) My mother bought yellow blankets yesterday.
6) They walked in the zoo for two hours.
7) I had to go to the doctor last week.
8) She shook the bottle of milk.
9) I put the answer at the top of the page.
10) She joked all evening.
11) We spent all the money very quickly.
12) You found a way to buy a car.
13) They saw a fire at the gas station.
14) I thought the bus stop was nearer.

ÊTRE = PAST TENSE

j'ai été
(I was, I've been)

≠ **je n'ai pas été**
(I wasn't, I haven't been)

tu as été
(you were, you've been)

≠ **tu n'as pas été**
(you weren't, you haven't been)

il
elle } **a été**
on

≠ **il**
elle } **n'a pas été**
on

he
(she } was, has been)
one

≠ he
(she } wasn't, hasn't been)
one

nous avons été
(we were, we've been)

≠ **nous n'avons pas été**
(we weren't, we haven't been)

vous avez été
(you were, you've been)

≠ **vous n'avez pas été**
(you weren't, you haven't been)

ils
elles } **ont été**
(they were, they've been)

≠ **ils**
elles } **n'ont pas été**
(they weren't, they haven't been)

Est-ce que tu as été malade hier?
Were you sick yesterday?

Oui, j'ai été malade hier.
Yes, I was ill yesterday.

Non, je n'ai pas été malade hier.
No, I wasn't sick yesterday.

translate:

1) I gave = ...
2) I thought = ...
3) I saw = ...
4) I answered = ...
5) I felt = ...
6) I took = ...
7) I read = ...
8) I paid = ...
9) I had to = ...
10) I called = ...
11) I ate = ...
12) I chose = ...
13) I opened = ...
14) I closed = ...

15) I drank = ...
16) I carried = ...
17) I heard = ...
18) I knew = ...
19) I made = ...
20) I slept = ...
21) I put = ...
22) I kept = ...
23) I wrote = ...
24) I hoped = ...
25) I ran = ...
26) I had = ...
27) I wanted = ...
28) I said = ...

VOCABULAIRE/VOCABULARY

	translation	synonym/ associated	opposite/ associated
1) (la) couverture	blanket	(le) drap = sheet	
2) (l')oreiller	pillow		
3) vraiment	really		
4) (le) bas	bottom		(le) haut = top
5) (le) cadeau	gift, present		
6) (un) feu	(a) fire	(l')incendie; (le) pompier = fireman	
7) (le) savon	soap	(la) serviette = towel	
8) /(la) gare /(l')arrêt de bus	/station (train)/bus stop		
9) (l')essence	petrol, gas	(la) station-service = filling, petrol or gas station	
10) appeler	to call	téléphoner = to phone	
11) (le) camion	lorry, truck		
12) plaisanter	to joke, kid	blaguer, (une) blague = joke = une plaisanterie	
13) (la) façon	way	(la) manière = manner	
14) /Allemagne /Italie	/Germany /Italy	allemand = German, italien = Italian	

Leçon 22/Lesson 22

PAST TENSE

Il est arrivé { hier / l'année dernière / il y a trois jours } = he arrived { yesterday / last year / three days ago }
(he has arrived)

careful! — some French verbs are conjugated with 'être'. Note that the past participle agrees with the subject:

example: il est arrivé, elle est arrivée, elles sont arrivées

---

je suis parti(e)

tu es parti(e)

il
elle } est parti(e)

on est parti

nous sommes parti(e)s

vous êtes parti(e)s

ils
elles } sont parti(e)s

Est-ce que tu <u>es allé</u> à Paris?	=	Did you go/Have you gone to Paris?
Oui, je <u>suis allé</u> à Paris.	=	Yes, I went/have gone to Paris.
Non, je <u>ne suis pas allé</u> à Paris.	=	No, I didn't go/haven't gone to Paris.

SOME VERBS CONJUGATED WITH 'ÊTRE'

ALLER → all<u>é</u>
(to go)

ARRIVER → arriv<u>é</u>
(to happen, to arrive)

DESCENDRE → descend<u>u</u>
(to go down)

DEVENIR → deven<u>u</u>
(to become)

ENTRER → entr<u>é</u>
(to come in)

MONTER → mont<u>é</u>
(to go up)

MOURIR → m<u>ort</u>
(to die)

NAÎTRE → n<u>é</u>
(to be born)

PARTIR → part<u>i</u>
(to leave)

RENTRER → rentr<u>é</u>
(to return)

RESTER → rest<u>é</u>
(to stay)

RETOURNER → retourn<u>é</u>
(to return)

REVENIR → reven<u>u</u>
(to come back)

SORTIR → sort<u>i</u>
(to go out)

TOMBER → tomb<u>é</u>
(to fall)

VENIR → ven<u>u</u>
(to come)

translate:

a   1) Mon grand-père est mort l'été dernier.
     2) Je suis né à New-York.
     3) Nous sommes restés deux semaines à l'hôtel.
     4) Pourquoi es-tu revenu si tôt?
     5) Ils sont allés en vacances à Noël.
     6) Nous sommes sortis samedi soir.

b   1) We left on time.
     2) She came into the store all alone.
     3) I fell in the street this morning.
     4) He went up to his room an hour ago.
     5) He became rich very quickly.
     6) At what time did you return?

DÉJÀ – PAS ENCORE = ALREADY – NOT YET

Est-ce qu'elle est déjà partie?	Has she already left? Has she left already?
Oui, elle est déjà partie.	Yes, she has already left.
Non, elle n'est pas encore partie.	No, she hasn't left yet.
Non, pas encore.	No, not yet.

translate:

a 1) Il a déjà cassé le cendrier.
   2) Ma soeur ne fume pas encore.
   3) Il est déjà venu ici.
   4) Il n'a pas encore répondu.

b 1) Has she already eaten?
   2) He hasn't called yet.
   3) That kind of thing happened already.
   4) He doesn't know how to dance yet.

VOCABULAIRE/VOCABULARY

	translation	synonym/ associated	opposite/ associated
1) (le) chocolat	chocolate		(la) vanille = vanilla
2) (la) cigarette	cigarette	(le) cigare = cigar, (la) pipe = pipe, (le) cendrier = ashtray, (l')allumette = match	
3) fumer	to smoke		
4) (le) cirque	circus	(le) clown = clown	
5) grimper	to climb		
6) entrer (dans)	to enter		
7) (la) conversation	conversation		
8) cuire	to cook	faire la cuisine = to do the cooking	
9) (le) coin	corner	au coin = on the corner	
10) danser	to dance	(la) danse = dance, (la) musique = music	
11) chanter	to sing	(le) disque = record, (la) chanson = song	
12) (l')endroit	place, spot	dans le coin = in the area	
13) des lunettes	glasses	(les) lentilles de contact = contact lenses	
14) arriver	to happen, occur	se passer, se produire	

Leçon 23/Lesson 23

PRESENT	PAST
Elle <u>travaille</u> ici depuis dix ans. (She's worked here/she's been working here for ten years.)	**Elle <u>a travaillé</u> ici dix ans.** (She worked here for ten years.)
Je t'<u>attends</u> depuis une heure. (I've been waiting for you for an hour.)	**Je t'<u>ai attendu</u> une heure.** (I waited for you for an hour.)
Elle <u>est divorcée</u> depuis cinq ans. (She's been divorced for five years.)	**Elle <u>a divorcé</u> il y a cinq ans.** (She divorced five years ago.)

careful! — remember this vital use of the French present

translate:

a 1) Je suis ici depuis six mois.
   2) Elle est restée une semaine à la campagne.
   3) Nous sommes en vacances depuis deux jours.
   4) Nous mangeons depuis deux heures.

b 1) We've been married for ten years, and I was married before for five years.
   2) I've been living here since Christmas, but before I lived in New York for eight years.
   3) The kids have been watching television for hours; yesterday, they watched only one hour.
   4) We've been talking for a long time. We talked for a long time last week too.

VENIR DE + INFINITIVE = TO (HAVE) JUST

Elle vient de prendre un bain.　　She just took a bath.
　　　　　　　　　　　　　　　　　　　(She's just taken a bath.)

Nous venons de manger.　　　　　We just ate.
　　　　　　　　　　　　　　　　　　　(We've just eaten.)

---

translate:

a　1) Je viens de voir mes grands-parents.
　　2) Je viens de lui écrire.
　　3) Je viens de les inviter.
　　4) Mon appareil-photo vient de casser.

b　1) My father has just left.
　　2) I just saw him an hour ago.
　　3) My brother just wrote to my sister.
　　4) She just called me an hour ago.

TOUS LES COMBIEN . . . ?

Vous prenez des cours de Français tous les combien?

HOW OFTEN . . . ?

How often do you take French lessons?

translate:

a 1) Tu vas au cinéma tous les combien?
   2) Vous partez en vacances tous les combien?

b 1) How often do you take a bath?
   2) How often do your parents go to the restaurant?

COMBIEN DE TEMPS . . . ?

Combien de temps êtes-vous resté?

HOW LONG . . . ?

How long did you stay?

translate:

a 1) Combien de temps pensez-vous rester?
   2) Combien de temps cela prendra-t-il?

b 1) How long did the trip take?
   2) How long did you talk with her?

127

1)	**pendant que**	while
	tandis que	
	pendant	during
	durant	
2)	**soudain**	suddenly
	tout à coup	all of a sudden
3)	**enfin**	at last
		finally
4)	**encore**	still
	toujours	
5)	**d'ici (samedi)**	by (Saturday)
6)	**définitivement**	for good
7)	**si**	if
	pourvu que	provided that
8)	**d'abord**	at first
9)	**partout**	all over, everywhere
	≠ **nulle part**	≠ nowhere
10)	**il est vraisemblable**	it's likely
	probablement	probably
	≠ **il est invraisemblable**	≠ it's unlikely

REVISION OF ADVERBS

list 1 — page 48, list 2 — page 75, list 3 — page 115, list 4 — page 123, list 5 — page 151

translate:

1) usually = . . .
2) at any rate = . . .
3) sometimes = . . .
4) often = . . .
5) seldom = . . .
6) at least = . . .
7) hardly = . . .
8) until = . . .
9) already = . . .
10) maybe = . . .
11) not yet = . . .
12) more or less = . . .
13) in the meanwhile = . . .
14) from time to time = . . .
15) instead of = . . .
16) in spite of = . . .
17) however = . . .
18) now and then = . . .
19) especially = . . .
20) on purpose = . . .
21) as soon as = . . .
22) not long ago = . . .
23) because of = . . .
24) since = . . .
25) for good = . . .
26) at last = . . .
27) suddenly = . . .
28) at first = . . .
29) it's likely = . . .
30) by (Saturday) = . . .

translate:

a 1) Il est vraisemblable qu'elle va venir.
2) Nous allons peut-être faire cuire le poulet.
3) Est-ce qu'ils vivent toujours en Allemagne?
4) Je ne pourrai pas faire mes devoirs d'ici lundi.
5) J'ai enfin compris.
6) Je l'aime encore.
7) Ils habiteront définitivement à Paris, pourvu qu'ils trouvent un appartement bon marché.
8) Mes parents t'inviteront probablement à dîner ce soir.

b 1) She came in suddenly.
2) At last I understand my parents.
3) I'll be able to do it by Saturday.
4) They're living in New York for good.
5) I looked all over for a watch like yours.
6) At first I didn't understand that she was tired.
7) He'll probably come tomorrow.
8) I'll come provided that you invite my best friend too.

VOCABULAIRE/VOCABULARY

	translation	synonym/ associated	opposite/ associated
1) Devine!	Guess!		
2) (un) rhume	(a) cold	(un) mal de gorge = sore throat	
3) (un) mal de tête	(a) headache		
4) important	important	sérieux, grave = serious	
5) (le) musée	museum	(le) monument = monument	
6) (le) bruit	noise		
7) /(le) boulanger /(le) boucher /(l')épicier	/baker/butcher /grocer	chez le boulanger = at/to the the baker's/the butcher's/the grocer's	
8) (le) parc	park		
9) (l')appareil-photo	camera	(la) pellicule, (le) film = camera film, (la) photographie = photograph	
10) décider	to decide	se décider = to make up one's mind	
11) délicieux	delicious		
12) inviter	to invite		
13) je me demande si	I wonder if		
14) (les) cheveux	hair	j'ai les cheveux châtains = my hair is brown	

Leçon 24/Lesson 24

> **EN TRAIN DE + INFINITIVE** = -ING, IN THE MIDST OF
>
> **Il est en train de manger.** He's (in the midst of) eating.

careful! — in French, you can translate 'we're watching television' either by 'nous regardons la télévision' or 'nous sommes en train de regarder la télévision'

translate:

a 1) Nous sommes en train de parler.
   2) Elle est en train de dormir.

b 1) She's eating an ice cream.
   2) They're in the midst of getting divorced.

> **ÊTRE SUR LE POINT DE + INFINITIVE ...** = TO BE ABOUT TO ...
>
> **Nous sommes sur le point de partir.** = We're about to leave.

translate:

a 1) Nous sommes sur le point de manger.
   2) Elle est sur le point d'aller se coucher.

b 1) She's about to wash her hair.
   2) We're about to drink a coffee.

AVOIR ENVIE DE . . .   =   TO FEEL LIKE . . .

J'ai <u>envie</u> $\begin{cases} \underline{d}'y \text{ aller.} \\ \underline{d}'un \text{ sandwich.} \end{cases}$ I <u>feel like</u> $\begin{cases} going. \\ a \text{ sandwich.} \end{cases}$

---

translate:

a   1) J'ai envie de voir ce film.
    2) J'ai envie d'un chocolat chaud.
    3) Est-ce que tu as envie d'aller te baigner?
    4) Nous n'avons pas envie de manger tout de suite.

b   1) Do you feel like an ice cream?
    2) My parents don't feel like going on vacation this summer.
    3) I don't feel like working this evening.
    4) She always feels like eating.

VOCABULAIRE/VOCABULARY

	translation	synonym/ associated	opposite/ associated
1) je te parie . . .	I bet you		
2) (la) balle	ball		
3) durer	to last		
4) /différent (de) /différence	/different (from) /difference	comme = like	le même (que) = the same as, semblable à = similar to
5) à droite	on the right		à gauche = on the left
6) (la) poche/(le) portefeuille	/pocket/wallet		
7) rêver	to dream	(un) rêve = dream	
8) tomber	to drop		ramasser = to pick up
9) connu	famous	célèbre	inconnu = unknown
10) (le) journal	newspaper	(le) magazine = magazine	
11) /(le) voyage /voyager	/trip/to travel	faire un voyage = to take a trip	
12) tenter	to attempt	essayer = to try	

VERBS AND PREPOSITIONS

a) fill in the blanks in the second column
b) fold the page back to check your answer
c) read the translation of the sentence for further clarification

1) to be . . . ing/ to be in the midst of . . . ing	**Je suis en train . . . me laver les cheveux.**
2) to talk to/ to speak with	**Est-ce que je peux parler . . . Anne?**
3) to be about to	**Nous sommes sur le point . . . sortir.**
4) What's it about?	**Je ne sais pas . . . quoi il s'agit.**
5) to need	**J'ai besoin . . . vous.**
6) to depend on/ to be up to	**Cela ne dépend pas . . . moi.**
7) to have just	**Elle vient . . . appeler.**
8) to feel like	**Qu'as-tu envie . . . faire ce soir?**

VERBS AND PREPOSITIONS

1) être en train de	I'm (in the midst of) washing my hair.
2) parler à	May I — talk to Anne? — speak with Anne?
3) être sur le point de	We're about to go out.
4) De quoi s'agit-il?	I don't know what it's about.
5) avoir besoin de	I need you.
6) dépendre de	It does not depend on me. It's not up to me.
7) venir de	She just called.
8) avoir envie de	What do you feel like doing tonight?

VERBS AND PREPOSITIONS

1) to be afraid of	J'ai peur . . . toi.
2) to be interested in	Je ne suis pas intéressé . . . ce que tu dis.
3) to be mad at	Pourquoi es-tu fâché . . . moi?
4) to explain something to someone	Expliquez ça . . . votre médecin.
5) on behalf of	J'appelle de la part . . . ma sœur.
6) to laugh at	Pourquoi vous moquez-vous . . . lui?
7) to belong to	. . . qui appartient la voiture bleue?
8) to plan to	J'ai l'intention . . . aller au cinéma.
9) to agree with	Mon père est d'accord . . . moi.

VERBS AND PREPOSITIONS

1) **avoir peur de**	I'm afraid of you.
2) **être intéressé par**	I'm not interested in what you're saying.
3) **être fâché contre**	What are you mad at?
4) **expliquer quelque chose à quelqu'un**	Explain that to your doctor.
5) **de la part de**	I'm calling on behalf of my sister.
6) **se moquer de**	Why are you laughing at him?
7) **appartenir à**	Who does the blue car belong to?
8) **avoir l'intention de**	I plan to go to the movies.
9) **être d'accord avec**	My father agrees with me.

IDIOMS

a) fill in the blanks in the second column as far as you can,
b) fold the page back to check your answer,
c) read the translation of the sentence for further clarification.

1) to go to bed	**Il est l'heure d'aller . . . . . .**
2) to go for a walk	**Je veux aller . . . . . .**
3) What a mess!	**Quelle . . . !**
4) What a fuss!	**Quelle . . . !**
5) to have (the) time	**Je n'aurai pas . . . de vous voir aujourd'hui.**
6) to do the dishes, wash up	**Vous devez faire . . . . . .**
7) /to be like/to resemble	**/Il . . . . . . sa mère./Il . . . . . . moi, il boit peu.**
8) to be right ≠ wrong	**Vous avez toujours . . . ≠ . . .**
9) It's a shame!/a pity!	**C'est . . . !**
10) Shut up!	**Fermez . . . !**
11) to take a trip	**Nous ferons . . . . . . cet été.**
12) /How are things?/Things aren't so great.	**/Ça . . . ?/Ça ne . . . . . . très bien.**
13) to be lucky	**J'ai eu beaucoup . . . . . .**

1) **aller se coucher**	It's time to go to bed.
2) **aller se promener**	I want to go for a walk.
3) **Quelle pagaille!**	What a mess!
4) **Quelle histoire!**	What a fuss!
5) **avoir le temps**	I won't have time to see you today.
6) **faire la vaisselle**	You have to do the dishes.
7) **/ressembler à/être comme**	/He is like his mother/He is like me, he drinks little.
8) **avoir raison ≠ avoir tort**	You're always right ≠ wrong.
9) **C'est dommage!**	It's — a shame! — a pity!
10) **Fermez-la!**	Shut up!
11) **faire un voyage**	We'll take a trip this summer.
12) **/Ça va?/Ça ne va pas très bien.**	/How are things?/Things aren't so great.
13) **avoir de la chance**	I've been very lucky.

IDIOMS

1) I'm pleased to meet you! | **...!**
2) Keep quiet! | **Restez ... !**
3) Be careful! | **Fais ... !**
4) I don't care. | **Ça lui ... ... !**
5) It doesn't matter! | **Cela ne ... ... !**
6) to change one's mind | **J'ai changé ... ...**
7) to do a favour | **Il ne m'a jamais ... ...**
8) to make up one's mind | **... ... ... vous!**
9) to queue, stand in line | **Il a fallu faire ... ...**
10) What's new? | **Quoi ... ... ?**
11) to be fed up/to have had it | **j'en ai ... ... / ...**

12) It's nice out. | **Il fait ...**
13) to be sorry | **Nous ... ...**

IDIOMS

1) **Enchanté!**	I'm pleased to meet you!
2) **Restez tranquilles!**	Keep quiet!
3) **Fais attention!**	Be careful!
4) **Ça m'est égal!**	He doesn't care!
5) **Cela ne fait rien!**	It doesn't matter!
6) **changer d'avis**	I changed my mind.
7) **rendre service**	He never did me a favour.
8) **se décider**	Make up your mind!
9) **faire la queue**	We have to queue up/stand in line
10) **Quoi de neuf?**	What's new?
11) **/en avoir ras le bol/en avoir marre.**	/I'm fed up/I've had it.
12) **Il fait beau.**	It's nice out.
13) **être désolé**	We're sorry.

IDIOMS

1) to make an appointment	**J'ai pris . . . pour ce soir.**
2) to make a mistake	**Je fais toujours beaucoup . . . . . .**
3) to make an effort	**Vous devez . . . . . .**
4) Too bad! ≠ All the better!	**Tant . . . ! ≠ Tant . . . !**
5) to look well	**Tu as très . . . . . .**
6) to hurt	**Cela ne . . . pas . . .**
7) /to take a test/to pass a test	**/Je dois . . . un examen demain. /Est-ce que vous avez . . . votre examen?**
8) as you like	**Comme . . . . . .**
9) to leave someone alone	**Laissez-moi . . . !**
10) to have a good time	**/Ils . . . sont . . . . . . /Amusez-vous . . . !**
11) to hurry up	**. . . -vous!**
12) to catch a cold	**J'ai attrapé . . . . . .**

IDIOMS

1) prendre rendez-vous	I made an appointment for tonight.
2) faire une faute	I always make many mistakes.
3) faire un effort	You have to make an effort.
4) Tant pis! ≠ Tant mieux!	Too bad! ≠ All the better!
5) avoir bonne mine	You look very well.
6) faire mal	It doesn't hurt.
7) /passer une examen/réussir un examen	/I have to take a test tomorrow. /Did you pass your test?
8) comme vous voulez	As you like.
9) laisser quelqu'un tranquille	Leave me alone!
10) bien s'amuser	They had a good time./Have a good time!
11) se dépêcher	Hurry up!
12) attraper un rhume	I caught a cold.

CONGRATULATIONS!

You are no longer a beginner. You can now go on to the more comprehensive French In No Time.

CORRIGÉ = KEY

Leçon 1, page 1

a 1) Are you French? — Yes, I'm French. 2) Are you sad? — Yes, I'm sad. 3) Are you sorry? — Yes, we're sorry. 4) Are you tall? — Yes, I'm tall.

b 1) Est-ce que tu es/vous êtes heureux? — Oui, je suis heureux. 2) Est-ce que tu es/vous êtes fatigué? — Oui, je suis fatigué. 3) Est-ce que tu es/vous êtes petit? — Oui, je suis petit. 4) Est-ce que tu es/vous êtes jeune? — Oui, je suis jeune.

Leçon 1, page 3

a 1) Excuse me, I'm sorry. 2) He's happy. 3) They're old. 4) We're young. 5) Is it blue? 6) Again? Yes, once more. 7) I'm tall. 8) You're American.

b 1) Comment allez-vous? 2) C'est laid. 3) Est-ce qu'elle est française? 4) Ils sont désolés. 5) Elle est petite. 6) Nous sommes heureux. 7) A bientôt! 8) Bonjour!

Leçon 2, page 6

a 1) What's wrong? 2) He isn't foolish. 3) It isn't warm. 4) They aren't doctors. 5) They aren't weak. 6) Do you understand? 7) It isn't long. 8) We aren't nurses.

b 1) Je ne suis pas stupide. 2) Ce n'est pas extra. 3) Tu n'es pas bête/Vous n'êtes pas bêtes. 4) Il n'est pas tôt. 5) Qu'est-ce qu'il y a? 6) Il n'est pas gentil. 7) Il n'est pas fort. 8) Merci. De rien.

Leçon 2, page 8

a 1) She's poor and I'm poor too. 2) He's boring and you're boring too. 3) He's ugly, but he's nice. 4) We're short and thin. 5) The books aren't expensive and they're new. 6) You're old and dirty too. 7) I'm young and beautiful. 8) The book isn't cheap, but it's beautiful.

b) 1) Je suis riche et elle est riche aussi. 2) Nous sommes forts et intelligents aussi. 3) Vous n'êtes pas sale/Tu n'es pas sale, mais il est sale. 4) Elle est jolie et vous êtes/tu es jolie aussi. 5) Il est grand et mince. 6) La leçon n'est pas facile, mais elle est intéressante. 7) L'infirmière est ici et le médecin aussi. 8) Ils ne sont pas chers, mais ils sont beaux.

Leçon 3, page 11

1) Est-ce que c'est un stylo noir? 2) Est-ce que c'est un téléphone bleu? 3) Est-ce que c'est une jeune infirmière? 4) Est-ce que c'est une montre chère? 5) Est-ce que c'est un livre intéressant? 6) C'est une table sale. 7) C'est une leçon facile. 8) Est-ce que c'est une voiture bon marché?

Leçon 3, page 13

1) de jolis livres 2) de petits garçons 3) des femmes intéressantes 4) de beaux garçons 5) de jeunes chiens 6) des leçons stupides 7) de mauvais médecins 8) des infirmières moches 9) des tables noires 10) des téléphones blancs 11) des crayons bleus 12) des réveils rouges 13) de gros chats 14) des gosses minces 15) des enfants difficiles 16) des murs sales 17) des vieux manteaux 18) de bons gâteaux 19) des boîtes laides 20) de petits stylos.

Leçon 3, page 14

1) Oui, les filles sont jeunes. — Non, les filles ne sont pas jeunes — Est-ce que la fille est jeune? 2) Oui, les manteaux sont noirs. — Non, les manteaux ne sont pas noirs — Est-ce que le manteau est noir? 3) Oui, les gâteaux sont durs. — Non, les gâteaux ne sont pas durs. — Est-ce que le gâteau est dur? 4) Oui, les chiens sont sous la table. — Non, les chiens ne sont pas sous la table. — Est-ce que le chien est sous la table? 5) Oui, les hommes sont riches. — Non, les hommes ne sont pas riches. — Est-ce que l'homme est riche? 6) Oui, les leçons sont dures. — Non, les leçons ne sont pas dures. — Est-ce que la leçon est dure? 7) Oui, les portes sont noires. — Non, les portes ne sont pas noires. — Est-ce que la porte est noire? 8) Oui, nous sommes ici. — Non, nous ne sommes pas ici. Est-ce que je suis ici? 9) Oui, les crayons sont blancs. — Non, les crayons ne sont pas blancs. Est-ce que le crayon est blanc? 10) Oui, les montres sont chères. — Non, les montres ne sont pas chères. — Est-ce que la montre est chère?

Leçon 3, page 16

a 1) Tuesday's after Monday. 2) You're late. 3) The young girl's beautiful. 4) The blue car's old. 5) The red table's far (away). 6) The cake's soft, but it's bad.

b 1) L'homme est intéressant et la femme est gentille. 2) Vous êtes/tu es en avance et je suis en retard. 3) Le restaurant est bon. 4) Vous êtes/Tu es méchant et elle aussi. 5) Le livre est difficile et les leçons sont dures. 6) Le type n'est pas vieux et la nana est jeune.

Leçon 4, page 19

1) Non, la robe n'est pas bon marché. — Non, les robes ne sont pas bon

marché.   2) Non, le sac n'est pas sur la table. — Non, les sacs ne sont pas sur la table.   3) Non, le type n'est pas jeune. — Non, les types ne sont pas jeunes.   4) Non, la femme n'est pas grosse. — Non, les femmes ne sont pas grosses.   5) Non, la leçon n'est pas difficile. — Non, les leçons ne sont pas difficiles.   6) Non, la chemise n'est pas noire. — Non, les chemises ne sont pas noires.   7) Non, je ne suis pas jeune. — Non, nous ne sommes pas jeunes. 8) Non, la veste n'est pas neuve. — Non, les vestes ne sont pas neuves. 9) Non, le mouchoir n'est pas sale. — Non, les mouchoirs ne sont pas sales. 10) Non, la jupe n'est pas courte. — Non, les jupes ne sont pas courtes.

Leçon 4, page 20

a 1) There are two hats on the chair.   2) There's a coat next to Jane. 3) There are four bags here.   4) There are two old men there.

b 1) Il y a une robe rouge sur la chaise.   2) Il y a un bébé à côté de la femme.   3) Il y a cinq vieux pulls ici.   4) Il y a une chemise bleue sous la table.

Leçon 4, page 21

a 1) It's a quarter to eight.   2) It's half-past one.   3) It's a quarter-past three.   4) It's two o'clock.   5) It's half-past five.

b 1) Il est deux heures et demie.   2) Il est quatre heures trente.   3) Il est huit heures et quart.   4) Il est six heures.   5) Il est cinq heures moins dix.

Leçon 4, page 22

belles — gentilles — blanche — grosse — bon — douces — chères — neuves — heureuse — fausse — longue — vieilles — première — malheureux — dernière — nouvelle — belle — favori — vieux — blanches

Leçon 5, page 25

a 1) The kids are lazy.   2) His bike is next to my car.   3) Your coat's awful.   4) Our bottle's old.   5) Your neck's long and dirty.   6) Their clothes are cheap and pretty too.

b) 1) Est-ce que ce sont vos voitures?   2) Son parapluie est joli. 3) Dimanche est mon jour favori.   4) Ses yeux sont beaux mais ses pieds sont laids.   5) Nos mains sont sales.   6) Leurs imperméables sont vieux.

Leçon 6, page 28

1) le mien   2) la leur   3) les nôtres   4) le sien   5) les siens   6) les miens 7) les tiens/les vôtres   8) les siennes   9) la nôtre   10) la mienne   11) le sien 12) les siennes   13) la mienne.

Leçon 6, page 29

a 1) Your mouth is small and mine is too. 2) Is it your plane? — Yes, it's mine. 3) Is it his/her car? — No, it isn't his/hers. 4) Is it our boat? — No, it isn't ours. 5) Our school's pretty and theirs is too. 6) Their subway's very dirty but ours is clean.

b 1) Est-ce que c'est ton/votre train? — Oui, c'est le mien. 2) Est-ce que ce sont ses boîtes? — Oui, ce sont les siennes. 3) Nos dents sont sales et les vôtres/tiennes aussi. 4) Ses pieds ne sont pas chauds, mais les miens le sont. 5) Leur professeur est gentil mais le nôtre ne l'est pas. 6) Ton/votre cours est difficile et le mien aussi.

Leçon 7, page 32

1) de la 2) des 3) de la 4) de l' 5) de la 6) de la 7) de 8) du 9) des 10) du 11) du 12) de l' 13) de l' 14) de l' 15) de 16) du 17) de la 18) de la 19) de la 20) du 21) du 22) de la 23) du 24) de l'

Leçon 7, page 33

a 1) Jane's eyes are blue. 2) The woman's bag is big. 3) Ann's umbrella is near the wall. 4) Peter's car is in front of the door. 5) Your cat is on the table and mine's on the chair. 6) The kid's book is under his arm but mine's next to me.

b 1) Le vélo d'Anne est vert. 2) Les étudiants du professeur sont paresseux. 3) L'école de Jean est près de la mienne. 4) Les dents de ma sœur sont sales. 5) La bouche de la fille est belle. 6) Les pieds de mon père sont grands.

Leçon 7, page 34

a 1) This plane's fast, but that boat's slow. 2) This girl's crazy. 3) This teacher's no good. 4) That book is awful.

b 1) Cet homme-là est mon père. 2) Cette maison est la mienne. 3) Cet hiver est dégueulasse. 4) Ce pull est le mien, mais ce col roulé-là est le tien.

Leçon 7, page 36

a 1) The chair isn't heavy and the table isn't either. 2) The glass is full and the bottle is too. 3) Are you upstairs? 4) Is a new house expensive? 5) I'm not first and you aren't either. 6) The boat's wide, but the plane isn't.

b 1) Il n'y a pas beaucoup d'avenues sûres à Paris. 2) Mon livre n'est pas épais, mais il est bon marché. 3) Ma sœur n'est pas en bas et ma mère non plus. 4) Il y a des tas de gens dans cette rue. 5) Mon vélo est bas et le tien aussi. 6) Ce bonbon n'est pas amer mais il est dur.

Leçon 8, page 39

a 1) The teacher has many stupid students. Est-ce que le professeur a beaucoup d'élèves stupides? 2) She has five knives, three forks and eight spoons. Est-ce qu'elle a cinq couteaux, trois fourchettes, et huit cuillers?
3) They have a few turtle-necks. Est-ce qu'ils ont quelques cols roulés.
4) We don't have a big house. Est-ce que nous avons une grande maison?
5) My sister has two children. Est-ce que ma sœur a deux enfants? 6) An hour has sixty minutes. Est-ce qu'une heure a soixante minutes?

b 1) Est-ce que vous avez neuf couteaux? 2) Chaque jour a vingt-quatre heures. 3) Est-ce qu'elle a une serviette? 4) Ce restaurant n'a pas de jolies assiettes. 5) Je suis sûre que l'école est très bonne. 6) Est-ce que vous avez/tu as un parapluie avec toi?

Leçon 8, page 41

a 1) I'm really late. 2) She's often tired in the evening. 3) You have almost ten francs and Jane (has) too. 4) I'm sometimes very happy.
5) We're always nice to our parents. 6) Everything's expensive except that cake.

b 1) Ils ont au moins 20 francs. 2) D'habitude, nous mangeons à la maison sauf les dimanches. 3) Elle a rarement son imperméable avec elle. 4) Nous avons presque quinze dollars. 5) Le restaurant a généralement du bon pain.
6) De toutes manières, mon professeur est très gentil.

Leçon 8, page 42

1) Je n'ai pas faim, mais j'ai soif. 2) De toutes façons, j'ai peur. 3) J'ai presque dix ans. 4) Je n'ai pas chaud mais je n'ai pas froid non plus.
5) Je suis sûr que vous avez/tu as raison. 6) Je n'ai pas tort et je suis content(e). 7) Tu as/vous avez de la chance! 8) As-tu/avez-vous sommeil?

Leçon 8, page 43

a 1) I'm in a hurry and Jane is too. 2) My father's seldom at work at 7 a.m.
3) We're usually very hungry in the evening. 4) In any case, you're not mean/nasty. 5) My mother and my father aren't always nice. 6) They're often cold in February in their house. 7) I'm very busy at noon. 8) She's alone one hour every day.

b 1) As-tu/avez-vous froid? 2) Tu as/vous avez toujours de la chance.
3) J'ai très peur mais pas elle. 4) Ma sœur a très sommeil et lui aussi.
5) Je suis sûr(e) que tu as/vous avez tort. 6) De toutes façons, tu as/vous avez toujours raison. 7) Je suis d'habitude à la maison à huit heures. 9) À qui est-ce le tour?

Leçon 9, page 46

a 1) Oui, d'habitude les enfants jouent tous les jours. — Non, d'habitude les enfants ne jouent pas tous les jours. 2) Oui, mon père travaille à la maison. — Non, mon père ne travaille pas à la maison. 3) Oui, il neige souvent en été. — Non, il ne neige pas souvent en été. 4) Oui, les enfants posent beaucoup de questions. — Non, les enfants ne posent pas beaucoup de questions. 5) Oui, nous mangeons souvent au restaurant. — Non, nous ne mangeons pas souvent au restaurant. 6) Oui, elle s'habille généralement seule. — Non, elle ne s'habille pas généralement seule.

b 1) I eat a lot of cakes every day. 2) I don't work with her/his brother. 3) You're asking too many questions. 4) It isn't snowing at the moment. 5) My sister gets dressed alone (by herself). 6) We talk a lot together.

Leçon 9, page 48

a 1) Are you going there today? 2) We're eating too many cakes. 3) My children often throw their clothes on the chair. 4) I hope to eat a lot at the restaurant tonight. 5) My parents always buy cheap toys. 6) Please, send me a new game.

b 1) Nous allons rarement à l'école à sept heures. 2) Nous commençons à comprendre la question. 3) D'habitude nous mangeons très tôt. 4) Ils envoient beaucoup de jouets aux gosses de leurs amis. 5) Il achète une nouvelle voiture. 6) Elle espère avoir un autre chien bientôt.

Leçon 9, page 49

a 1) Que demandez-vous? 2) Qui mange avec vous ce soir? 3) Qui joue avec votre sœur? 4) Qu'achètent-ils?

b 1) I'm speaking to my brother. 2) I often think about you. 3) I sometimes go to the restaurant. 4) Show your new bike to your father.

Leçon 10, page 52

1) Est-ce qu'ils choisissent une nouvelle maison? 2) Elle finit son déjeuner. 3) Nous choisissons un nouveau chien. 4) Vous finissez avant moi.

Leçon 10, page 53

a 1) Who lives in this pretty house? 2) What are you putting in your bag? 3) Who gives you money every week? 4) What do you know? 5) The teacher whom(that) I meet every day is nice. 6) The clothes that (which) Mummy buys are beautiful.

b 1) Les enfants qui travaillent trop sont malheureux. 2) Le vélo que tu achètes est cher. 3) Le grand magasin que vous cherchez est très loin. 4) J'habite (dans) une maison qui est très jolie. 5) Vous avez besoin d'argent, il est sur la table. 6) La femme qui travaille dans ce magasin-là est ma tante.

Leçon 10, page 54

1) quel 2) quel 3) quel 4) quel 5) quel 6) quel 7) quelle 8) quel
9) quelle 10) quelles 11) quels 12) quel 13) quel 14) quel 15) quelle
16) quel 17) quelle 18) quelle 19) quel 20) quel 21) quelles 22) quel
23) quel 24) quelles 25) quel 26) quelle 27) quel 28) quelle 29) quelle
30) quels 31) quels 32) quel

Leçon 11, page 58

a 1) Don't answer now. 2) Do you know my brother? 3) What are you doing? 4) I've been living in Paris for two years. 5) My parents sleep together. 6) He often writes to me.

b 2) Nous partons cet après-midi à cinq heures. 2) D'habitude j'écris à ma grand-mère toutes les semaines. 3) Pourquoi courez-vous? 4) Je sors souvent sans mes parents. 5) Ouvrez la fenêtre, s'il vous plaît. 6) Pourquoi riez-vous?

Leçon 11, page 60

a 1) I always sit next to my pal. 2) I almost always eat meat for lunch.
3) I don't understand why you need this book. 4) I see my friends every day. 5) I don't know my lesson. 6) We can't watch television tonight.

b 1) Je veux voir mes amis tous les jours. 2) Viens et assieds-toi à côté de moi! 3) Nous buvons beaucoup de lait tous les jours. 4) Mets le poulet sur la table. 5) Dites-moi pourquoi vous êtes en retard. 6) Quel livre lisez-vous?

Leçon 12, page 62

a 1) We must speak French. 2) We mustn't speak during the lesson. 3) Do we have to pay right now? 4) You mustn't drink too much milk.

b 1) Il faut manger tous les jours. 2) Est-ce qu'il faut partir maintenant?
3) Il ne faut pas manger cela. 4) J'ai faim, nous devons acheter quelque chose à manger.

Leçon 12, page 64

a 1) I'm hardly hungry. 2) The waiter's rather intelligent. 3) Between French fries and string beans (runner beans), I want string beans.
4) Maybe the fish is good here. 5) You're quite right. 6) I don't want to work till six o'clock.

b 1) Nous avons à peine assez de pain pour le dîner. 2) Je suis occupé jusqu'à trois heures. 3) Cela ne fait rien, nous avons plus ou moins assez

d'argent. 4) Le serveur veut un gros pourboire comme d'habitude.
5) Combien est-ce que ça coûte environ? 6) Enfin, l'addition est là.

Leçon 13, page 66

seulement − vite − drôlement − bon − facilement − stupidement −
rarement − malheureusement − simplement − doucement − lentement −
mal − heureusement − vraiment − généralement − durement − difficilement
− dangereusement − profondément − bêtement − certainement

Leçon 13, page 67

a 1) He hopes (that) he's right. 2) I think (that) you're lucky. 3) I know
(that) he needs money. 4) I've the feeling (that) you're sad.

b 1) Sais-tu/savez-vous qu'il a une nouvelle voiture? 2) Ne dis/dites pas
à ta/votre mère que j'ai faim. 3) Je ne suis pas sûr que le magasin est
ouvert. 4) Nous espérons que cette erreur est la seule.

Leçon 13, page 68

a 1) She wants what I have. 2) It's not what I usually eat. 3) I know what
you want. 4) Eat what you can.

b 1) Est-ce que vous comprenez ce qu'elle dit? 2) Ce n'est pas ce que je
veux. 3) Est-ce que tu sais ce que ton grand-père pense? 4) Ses petits-
enfants disent qu'il est très vieux.

Leçon 13, page 70

a 1) Her daughter isn't often good. 2) Is my sweater dry? 3) The
bedroom's a mess. 4) Do you think they're brothers? 5) He isn't right.
6) She thinks that her kids are naughty.

b 1) Est-ce que c'est vrai ce truc? Bien sûr que non! 2) Mon beau-père est
souvent injuste. 3) Tu as un vilain frère. 4) Elle a envie d'une glace. Je suis
pour. 5) Mon père est toujours très poli. 5) Ta chambre est en pagaille
aujourd'hui.

Leçon 13, page 71

1) pauvre ≠ riche   2) laid ≠ beau   3) jeune ≠ vieux   4) gros ≠ mince
5) ennuyeux ≠ intéressant/passionnant   6) ici ≠ là   7) faible ≠ fort
8) rapide ≠ lent   9) dur ≠ mou   10) après ≠ avant   11) mauvais ≠ bon
12) gentil ≠ méchant/vilain   13) loin ≠ près   14) court ≠ long   15) petit ≠
grand   16) sale ≠ propre   17) en avance ≠ en retard   18) froid ≠ chaud/
très chaud   19) vilain ≠ sage   20) en bas ≠ en haut   21) plein ≠ vide
22) haut ≠ bas   23) dangereux ≠ sûr   24) étroit ≠ large   25) lourd ≠ léger
26) cher ≠ bon marché   27) premier ≠ dernier   28) injuste ≠ juste

29) profond ≠ peu profond   30) poli ≠ grossier   31) sec ≠ mouillé
32) contre ≠ pour   33) faux ≠ vrai   34) en pagaille ≠ rangé   35) vrai ≠
faux   36) épais ≠ mince   37) neuf/nouveau ≠ ancien   38) sucré ≠ amer, aigre

Leçon 14, page 74

a 1) I know her well.   2) She doesn't have it any more.   3) I don't hear
you.   4) I often see him.

b 1) Est-ce que tu me vois?   2) Écris-la vite.   3) Ne le bois pas!   4) Je ne te
crois pas.

Leçon 14, page 75

a 1) There's a lot of furniture in the apartment.   2) Your kitchen isn't
pretty.   3) The bathroom's dirty.   4) The curtains are too long.   5) Your
bedroom's too small.   6) Do you need to go to the bathroom?

b 1) L'ascenseur ne marche pas.   2) Écris-moi une lettre bientôt.   3) Le
placard est très haut.   4) Est-ce que vous avez besoin de timbres?   5) Notre
salle à manger est très grande.   6) Mon lit est dans le salon.

Leçon 14, page 78

1) S'il te plaît, envoie-moi un gâteau.   2) Je peux lui montrer le livre ce soir.
3) Dites-moi la vérité.   4) Ne leur réponds pas.   5) Écris-moi une lettre tous
les jours.   6) Je te parle.

Leçon 14, page 79

1) Do you often think about me?   2) She always tells me everything.
3) This dog doesn't belong to them.   4) My parents don't talk to him.
5) Write me what you think.   6) Give her your bike.

Leçon 15, page 81

a 1) Oui, je viendrai demain. — Non, je ne viendrai pas demain.   2) Oui, ils
prendront l'avion pour Chicago. — Non, ils ne prendront pas l'avion pour
Chicago.   3) Oui, je lui dirai pourquoi il a tort. — Non, je ne lui dirai pas
pourquoi il a tort.   4) Oui, il aura faim quand il partira. — Non, il n'aura
pas faim quand il partira.   5) Oui, elle ira en Angleterre la semaine
prochaine. — Non, elle n'ira pas en Angleterre la semaine prochaine.   6) Oui,
nous irons faire des courses samedi prochain. — Non, nous n'irons pas faire
des courses samedi prochain.   7) Oui, je pourrai t'aider demain. — Non, je ne
pourrai pas t'aider demain.   8) Oui, j'irai me coucher dans une heure. — Non,
je n'irai pas me coucher dans une heure.

b 1) J'essaierai de le voir la semaine prochaine.   2) Il mangera avec moi
demain.   3) Nous étudierons ensemble (pendant) ce week-end.   4) Elle nous

fera un gros gâteau ce soir. 5) Mon père ira à Londres dans une semaine.
6) Ils devront bientôt parler au professeur. 7) Je jouerai avec toi avant le
dîner. 8) Est-ce que tu iras au lit après moi?

Leçon 15, page 83

a 1) What will you do tomorrow? 2) She'll say no. 3) We'll play tennis
together in a week. 4) I'll do it next week. 5) We'll see our grandparents
tomorrow. 6) I'll drink a lot of milk tonight. 7) She won't leave the
hospital until Christmas. 8) I won't open the door.

b 1) Je prendrai mes vacances le mois prochain. 2) Je pourrai te voir dans
une semaine. 3) Qu'est-ce que vous ferez demain? 4) Mes parents
achèteront un nouveau bateau la semaine prochaine. 5) Ils l'appelleront
dans une semaine. 6) Nous commencerons le travail l'année prochaine.
7) Ils mettront la piscine devant la maison. 8) Nous nous assoirons sur le
divan.

Leçon 16, page 86

1) Si je t'apporte un gâteau, est-ce que tu le mangeras? 2) Si elle casse une
assiette, est-ce que tu la paieras? 3) Si nous avons beaucoup d'argent, est-ce
que nous irons faire des courses? 4) Si elle a faim, elle déjeunera. 5) Si tu
as soif, je te donnerai un verre de lait. 6) Si vous avez très chaud, est-ce que
vous irez vous baigner? 7) Si elle ne sait pas faire ses devoirs toute seule,
est-ce que tu l'aideras? 8) Si le zoo est sale, les animaux seront malades.
9) Si le lit est confortable, elle dormira dessus. 10) Si tu as un nouvel
animal, est-ce que tu me le montreras? 11) Si nous allons à la montagne,
nous irons faire du ski. 12) Si ils partent en vacances, est-ce que ce sera à
Noël? 13) S'il n'est pas bien, il restera au lit. 14) Si elle n'est plus malade,
nous jouerons au tennis demain.

Leçon 16, page 87

1) If the meal's cold, I'll be very pleased. Si le repas n'est pas froid, je ne
serai pas très contente. 2) If the bird's sick/ill, I'll be unhappy. Si l'oiseau
n'est pas malade, je ne serai pas triste. 3) If the beach's dirty, I'll go to the
forest. Si la plage n'est pas sale, je n'irai pas dans la forêt. 4) If you break
your leg, will you stay in bed? Si tu ne casses pas la jambe, est-ce que tu
resteras au lit? 5) If everybody's hungry, we'll eat early. Si personne n'a
faim, nous ne mangerons pas tôt. 6) If you come, we'll go out. Si tu ne
viens pas, nous ne sortirons pas. 7) What will you do if I'm sick/ill? Qu'est-
ce que tu feras si je ne suis pas malade? 8) Shall we/Will we go on vacation
if we have a lot of money? Est-ce que nous irons en vacances si nous n'avons
pas beaucoup d'argent? 9) If it rains, shall we/will we go to the beach? S'il
ne pleut pas, est-ce que nous irons à la plage? 10) If my favourite/best
friend goes, I'll go too. Si mon ami préféré n'y a va pas, je n'irai pas non plus.

11) If we go to the zoo this afternoon, we'll see monkeys, bears and snakes. Si nous n'allons pas au zoo cet après-midi, nous ne verrons pas de singes, d'ours et de serpents. 12) If you have to go to the doctor, will you take the train? Si tu n'as pas à aller chez le médecin, est-ce que tu prendras le train? 13) Even if you think he's stupid, don't say anything. Même si tu ne penses pas qu'il est bête, ne dis rien. 14) If you show me your homework, I'll show you mine. Si tu ne me montres pas tes devoirs, je ne te montrerai pas les miens.

Leçon 17, page 89

a 1) Est-ce qu'il arrive que votre voisin parte en vacances? — Non, mon voisin ne part jamais en vacances. 2) Est-ce qu'il vous arrive de manger des citrons? — Non, je ne mange jamais de citrons. 3) Est-ce qu'il lui arrive de prendre un bain le soir? — Non, elle ne prend jamais de bain le soir.
4) Est-ce qu'il leur arrive d'acheter des fleurs? — Non, ils n'achètent jamais de fleurs.

b 1) My parents' gardener never drinks beer. 2) Does your mother ever drink coffee? 3) Are you ever late? 4) I never put salt on apples.

Leçon 17, page 90

1) I've been eating for 15 minutes. 2) We've been married since February.
3) She's been talking for one hour. 4) The children are sleeping now.
5) Children sleep a lot. 6) The children have been sleeping for half-an-hour.

Leçon 17, page 91

a 1) Are you going to go to the beach this afternoon? 2) We're going to eat fruit tonight. 3) I'm going to take a bath at nine. 4) He isn't going to put any sugar in his milk.

b 1) Est-ce que vous allez venir ce soir? 2) Elle va prendre l'ascenseur.
3) Est-ce qu'ils vont acheter ce truc étrange? 4) J'espère que tu vas nous aider.

Leçon 17, page 92

a 1) The teacher has been speaking for an hour. 2) I've been here since January. 3) Do the children ever drink wine? 4) I'm going to the farm and I'm going to buy some milk. 5) Since when have you been going to school?
6) We are going to write letters tonight.

b 1) Je le connais depuis dix ans. 2) Mes parents ne boivent jamais de vin.
3) Nous habitons à New-York depuis huit mois. 4) Elle mange maintenant. Elle mange toujours à huit heures. 5) Est-ce qu'il vous arrive de prendre une douche le matin? 6) Vous parlez depuis une heure. Vous parlez toujours trop.

Leçon 18, page 94

a 1) I'm drinking (some) water. 2) She rarely eats sugar. 3) Does she have some chocolate? 4) We don't have any novels to read this summer.

b 1) Je veux de l'argent tout de suite. 2) Je ne bois jamais de café. 3) Est-ce que tu auras besoin d'aide? 4) Je n'ai pas de meubles dans ma chambre.

Leçon 18, page 95

a 1) I don't want any. 2) Do you have some? 3) I never eat any. 4) Do you want some?

b 1) Est-ce qu'elle en veut? 2) J'ai envie de chocolat, mais je n'en ai pas. 3) Pourquoi est-ce que tu n'en achètes pas? 4) Est-ce que tu es sûr que tu n'en as pas besoin?

Leçon 18, page 96

a 1) We have a few good pals. 2) She has a little money in her bag.
3) Do you need a few books for the vacation? 4) There's a little milk in the fridge.

b 1) J'ai seulement un peu d'argent. 2) La France n'a que quelques bonnes actrices. 3) L'histoire a seulement quelques pages. 4) L'Angleterre a très peu d'aéroports.

Leçon 18, page 98

a 1) Instead of spending your money, keep it. 2) In spite of the rain, we'll go for a walk. 3) We'll eat in the meantime. 4) It's too expensive, I can't buy it. 5) The story's interesting, however, the movie's bad. 6) I am at the airport in order to take a plane.

b 1) De temps en temps, nous allons aux États-Unis. 2) Il travaille dur afin d'aider ses parents. 3) Parle lentement et je te comprendrai. 4) C'est exactement ce que je veux. 5) Il est très gentil, pourtant je ne l'aime pas. 6) De temps à autre nous allons au restaurant.

Leçon 19, page 101

a 1) I'm taller than my mother. 2) His bike is more expensive than yours. 3) I find him funnier than usual. 4) He's the tallest in the class. 5) He's losing more money than I am. 6) I love him more than his sister.

b 1) Votre chien est plus laid que le mien. 2) Elle est la plus jolie de la famille. 3) C'est l'homme le plus riche du pays. 4) Vous êtes la personne la plus bête ici. 5) Elle est plus gentille que son professeur. 6) Le livre est plus intéressant que le film.

158

Leçon 19, page 103

a 1) This car is more expensive than the other one. 2) Is it the least expensive restaurant you know? 3) She doesn't believe that her grandmother is less intelligent than her grandfather. 4) I have more money than you do. 5) He's worse than his brother. 6) I think (find) that this actor is better than the others.

b 1) Qui est le professeur le plus intéressant de ton école? 2) Je pense que c'est le meilleur film de l'année. 3) Tu es la personne la pire. 4) Elle n'est pas aussi belle que sa sœur. 5) La France est presque aussi grande que l'Allemagne. 6) Cet acteur n'est pas aussi bon que son frère.

Leçon 19, page 105

a 1) Since you can't come, I'll come. 2) I'm glad because you're here. 3) Do it at once. 4) Above all, don't forget my birthday. 5) I did not do it on purpose. 6) I want to win once.

b 1) Puisque tu es là commençons le petit déjeuner. 2) A cause de la pluie, nous resterons à la maison. 3) Dès qu'il t'ecrira, dis-le moi. 4) Puisqu'il pleut, prends un parapluie. 5) Je l'achèterai plus tard. 6) J'aime bien sa famille, surtout sa mère.

Leçon 20, page 107

a 1) She still remembers him. 2) I don't live in England any more. 3) We don't want to leave any longer. 4) She still doesn't know how to get dressed on her own (alone).

b 1) Elle a encore peur de son père. 2) Est-ce qu'ils habitent toujours Londres? 3) Il ne fume plus. 4) Je ne veux plus aller à l'école.

Leçon 20, page 108

1) These coats are wet and those umbrellas are dry. 2) These shoes are mine. Are those boots yours? 3) These dogs aren't hers, but those cats are hers. 4) Those people aren't very nice.

Leçon 20, page 109

a 1) I don't know that movie. 2) I don't know how to speak French. 3) Do you know my brother? 4) I don't know my lesson any more. 5) I don't know London. 6) Do you know if he'll come?

b 1) Il ne sait pas la réponse. 2) Je ne connais pas ce magasin. 3) Ma mère sait conduire. 4) Elle ne connaît pas Pierre. 5) Elle ne sait pas que je viens. 6) Il ne connaît pas ce livre.

Leçon 21, page 112

a 1) They stopped working at six o'clock. 2) She paid ten dollars for this thing. 3) The waiter gave us the bill (check) an hour ago. 4) I called you last night. 5) You slept in the truck yesterday. 6) The school closed two days ago and everybody's on the beach.

b 1) Est-ce que vous avez dû aller à l'école à Pâques? 2) Nous avons donné un beau livre d'art à nos parents. 3) Le garçon nous a apporté des frites avec la viande. 4) Il m'a téléphoné hier. 5) J'ai mangé un pamplemousse et une poire il y a une heure. 6) J'ai entendu ma mère pleurer la semaine dernière.

Leçon 21, page 115

a 1) Est-ce qu'il a dépensé beaucoup d'argent? Non, il n'a pas dépensé beaucoup d'argent. 2) Est-ce que tu l'as fait avec ton frère? Non, je ne l'ai pas fait avec mon frère. 3) Est-ce que vous avez rencontré ces gens gentils? Non, nous n'avons pas rencontré ces gens gentils. 4) Est-ce que tu as été en Angleterre la semaine dernière. Non, je n'ai pas été en Angleterre la semaine dernière. 5) Est-ce qu'ils lui ont donné des fleurs? Non, ils ne lui ont pas donné de fleurs. 6) Est-ce qu'elle a acheté un nouveau manteau la semaine dernière? Non, elle n'a pas acheté de nouveau manteau la semaine dernière.

b 1) We hid the gift in the cupboard (closet). Est-ce que nous avons caché le cadeau dans le placard? 2) I talked to her yesterday. Est-ce que je lui ai parlé hier? 3) She tore her dress an hour ago. Est-ce qu'elle a déchiré sa robe il y a une heure? 4) The teacher stopped teaching a year ago. Est-ce que le professeur a arrêté d'enseigner il y a un an? 5) You had to go early because of the snow. Est-ce que vous avez dû partir tôt à cause de la neige? 6) You wrote to your grand-mother last summer. Est-ce que tu as écrit à ta grand-mère l'été dernier?

Leçon 21, page 116

1) Il a eu besoin d'argent hier soir. Est-ce qu'il a eu besoin d'argent hier soir? Non, il n'a pas eu besoin d'argent hier soir. 2) Il m'a appelé tard hier. Est-ce qu'il t'a appelé tard hier? Non, il ne m'a pas appelé tard hier. 3) Il m'a montré son nouvel animal domestique dimanche dernier. Est-ce qu'il t'a montré son nouvel animal domestique dimanche dernier? Non, il ne m'a pas montré son nouvel animal domestique dimanche dernier. 4) Nous lui avons donné un cadeau pour son anniversaire. Est-ce que vous lui avez donné un cadeau pour son anniversaire? Non, nous ne lui avons pas donné de cadeau pour son anniversaire. 5) Ma mère a acheté des couvertures jaunes hier. Est-ce que ta mère a acheté des couvertures jaunes hier? Non, ma mère n'a pas acheté de couvertures jaunes hier. 6) Ils ont marché dans le zoo pendant deux heures. Est-ce qu'ils ont marché dans le zoo pendant deux heures? Non, ils n'ont pas marché dans le zoo pendant deux heures. 7) J'ai dû aller chez le médecin la semaine dernière. Est-ce que vous avez dû aller chez le médecin

la semaine dernière? Non, je n'ai pas dû aller chez le médecin la semaine
dernière.   8) Elle a secoué la bouteille de lait. Est-ce qu'elle a secoué la
bouteille de lait? Non, elle n'a pas secoué la bouteille de lait.   9) J'ai mis la
réponse en haut de la page. Est-ce que tu as mis la réponse en haut de la page.
Non, je n'ai pas mis la réponse en haut de la page.   10) Elle a blagué toute la
soirée. Est-ce qu'elle a blagué toute la soirée? Non, elle n'a pas blagué toute la
soirée.   11) Nous avons dépensé tout l'argent très rapidement. Est-ce que
nous avons dépensé tout l'argent très rapidement? Non, nous n'avons pas
dépensé tout l'argent très rapidement.   12) Vous avez trouvé le moyen
d'acheter une voiture. Est-ce que vous avez trouvé le moyen d'acheter une
voiture? Non, je n'ai pas trouvé le moyen d'acheter une voiture.   13) Ils ont
vu un incendie à la station-service. Est-ce qu'ils ont vu un incendie à la
station-service? Non, ils n'ont pas vu d'incendie à la station-service.   14) Je
pensais que l'arrêt d'autobus était plus près. Est-ce que tu pensais que l'arrêt
d'autobus était plus près? Non, je ne pensais pas que l'arrêt d'autobus était
plus près.

Leçon 21, page 118

1) j'ai donné   2) j'ai pensé   3) j'ai vu   4) j'ai répondu   5) j'ai senti   6) j'ai
pris   7) j'ai lu   8) j'ai payé   9) j'ai dû   10) j'ai appelé   11) j'ai mangé
12) j'ai choisi   13) j'ai ouvert   14) j'ai fermé   15) j'ai bu   16) j'ai porté
17) j'ai entendu   18) j'ai su/connu   19) j'ai fait   20) j'ai dormi   21) j'ai mis
22) j'ai gardé   23) j'ai écrit   24) j'ai espéré   25) j'ai couru   26) j'ai eu
27) j'ai voulu   28) j'ai dit

Leçon 22, page 122

a 1) My grandfather died last summer.   2) I was born in New York.   3) We
stayed three weeks at the hotel.   4) Why did you come back so early?
5) They went on vacation at Christmas.   6) We went out Saturday evening.

b 1) Nous sommes partis à l'heure.   2) Elle est entrée dans le magasin
toute seule.   3) Je suis tombé dans la rue ce matin.   4) Il est monté dans sa
chambre il y a une heure.   5) Il est devenu riche très vite.   6) A quelle heure
êtes-vous rentrés?

Leçon 22, page 123

a 1) He has already broken the ashtray.   2) My sister doesn't smoke yet.
3) He's already come here.   4) He hasn't answered yet.

b 1) Est-ce qu'elle a déjà mangé?   2) Il n'a pas encore appelé.   3) Ce genre
de chose est déjà arrivé.   4) Il ne sait pas encore danser.

Leçon 23, page 125

a 1) I have been here for six months.   2) She stayed a week in the country.

3) We've been on vacation for two days.   4) We've been eating for two hours.

b 1) Nous sommes mariés depuis dix ans, mais j'ai été marié avant pendant cinq ans. 2) J'habite ici depuis Noël, mais avant, j'ai habité New-York pendant huit ans. 3) Les gosses regardent la télévision depuis des heures. Hier, ils l'ont regardé seulement une heure. 4) Nous parlons depuis longtemps. Nous avons parlé longtemps la semaine dernière aussi.

Leçon 23, page 126

a 1) I've just seen my grandparents. 2) I've just written to him. 3) I just invited them. 4) My camera just broke.

b 1) Mon père vient de partir. 2) Je viens de le voir il y a une heure.
3) Mon frère vient d'écrire à ma soeur. 4) Elle vient de m'appeler il y a une heure.

Leçon 23, page 127

a 1) How often do you go to the movies? 2) How often do you go on vacation?

b 1) Tu prends un bain tous les combien? 2) Tes parents vont au restaurant tous les combien?

Leçon 23, page 127

a 1) How long do you think you'll stay? 2) How long will it take?

b 1) Combien de temps a pris le voyage? 2) Combien de temps as-tu parlé avec elle?

Leçon 23, page 129

1) d'habitude 2) de toutes façons 3) parfois 4) souvent 5) rarement
6) au moins 7) à peine 8) jusqu'à 9) déjà 10) peut-être 11) pas encore
12) plus ou moins 13) entre-temps 14) de temps en temps 15) au lieu de
16) malgé 17) cependant 18) de temps à autre 19) surtout 20) exprès
21) dès que 22) il n'y pas longtemps 23) à cause de 24) puisque 25) dé-finitivement 26) enfin 27) soudain 28) d'abord 29) il est vraisemblable
30) d'ici (samedi)

Leçon 23, page 130

a 1) It's likely she's going to come. 2) Maybe, we're going to cook the chicken. 3) Do they still live in Germany? 4) I won't be able to do my homework by Monday. 5) At last I understood. 6) I still love him.
7) They'll live in Paris for good, provided that they find a cheap apartment.
8) My parents will probably invite you for dinner tonight.

b 1) Soudain elle est entrée.   2) Je comprends enfin mes parents.   3) Je pourrai le faire d'ici samedi.   4) Ils habitent définitivement New-York. 5) J'ai cherché partout une montre comme la tienne.   6) D'abord je n'ai pas compris qu'elle était fatiguée.   7) Il viendra probablement demain.   8) Je viendrai pourvu que tu invites aussi mon meilleur ami.

Leçon 24, page 132

a 1) We're talking.   2) She's sleeping.

b 1) Elle est en train de manger une glace.   2) Ils sont en train de divorcer.

Leçon 24, page 132

a 1) We're about to eat.   2) She's about to go to bed.

b 1) Elle est sur le point de se laver les cheveux.   2) Nous sommes sur le point de boire un café.

Leçon 24, page 133

a 1) I feel like seeing this movie.   2) I feel like a hot chocolate.   3) Do you feel like going swimming?   4) We don't feel like eating right now.

b 1) Est-ce que tu as envie d'une glace?   2) Mes parents n'ont pas envie de partir en vacances cet été.   3) Je n'ai pas envie de travailler ce soir.   4) Elle a toujours envie de manger.

VOCABULARY

a
a [has]
a acheté [bought]
a appelé [called]
a apporté [brought]
a appris [learned]
a arrêté [quit/stopped]
a attendu [waited]
a attrapé [caught]
abandonner [to give up]
à bientôt [see you soon]
absolument [absolutely]
a bu [drank]
a caché [hid]
a cassé [broke]
à cause de [because of]
acheter [to buy]
a choisi [chose]
a commencé [began/started]
a compris [understood]
a conduit [drove]
a connu [knew]
a continué [continued]
à côté de [next to]
a coupé [cut]
a couru [ran]
a coûté [cost]
acteur [actor] (m)
actrice [actress] (f)
addition [bill/check] (f)
a déchiré [tore]
a dépensé [spent]
a dit [said/told]
a donné [gave]
a dormi [slept]
à droite [on the right]
a dû [had to]
a écrit [wrote]
a enseigné [taught]
a entendu [heard]
a envoyé [sent]
aéroport [airport] (m)

a espéré [hoped]
a été [was]
a eu [had]
a eu besoin de [needed]
a eu l'impression de [felt]
a fait [made/did]
a fait mal [hurt]
a fermé [shut/closed]
affreux [awful]
afin de [so as to]
a fini [finished]
a gardé [kept]
agent de police [policeman](m)
agneau [lamb](m)
à (huit heures) [at (8 o'clock)]
a habité [lived]
ai (j') [have (I)]
aider [to help]
aigre [sour]
aimer [to love]
aimer bien [to like/to be fond of]
a jeté [threw]
a joué [played]
a laissé [let]
à la maison [at home]
à l'école [at school]
à l'heure [on time]
Allemagne [Germany] (f)
allemand [German]
aller [to go]
aller (faire) [to be going to . . .]
aller à [to go to]
aller nager [to go swimming]
aller se baigner [to go swimming]
aller se coucher [to go to bed]
aller se promener [to go for a walk]
allez-y! [go ahead!]
allumer [to turn on/to put on]
allumette [match] (f)
a lu [read]
a mangé [ate]
amer [bitter]

165

américain [American]
ami [friend] (m)
a mis [put]
ampoule [bulb] (f)
amusant [amusing]
anglais [English]
Angleterre [England] (f)
animal [animal] (m)
animal domestique [pet] (m)
année [year] (f)
anniversaire [birthday] (m)
a obtenu [got]
août [August]
a ouvert [opened]
a parié [bet]
a parlé [spoke/talked]
a payé [paid]
à peine [barely/hardly/scarcely]
a pensé [thought]
a peu près [almost/nearly]
à point [medium]
a porté [wore/carried]
appareil-photo [camera] (m)
appartement [flat,
    apartment] (m)
appartenir à [to belong to]
appeler [to call]
apporter [to bring]
apprendre [to learn]
après [after]
après-midi [afternoon] (m)
a prêté [lent]
a pris [took]
a pu [could/was able to]
à qui? [whose?]
a raconté [told]
arbre [tree] (m)
a reçu [got]
a regardé [watched]
a rencontré [met]
a répondu [answered]
argent [money] (m)
a ri [laughed]
arrêt de bus [bus stop] (m)
arrêter [to stop]
arriver [to occur/to

happen/to arrive]
artiste [artist] (m/f)
as (tu)? [have (you)] ?
ascenseur [elevator/lift] (m)
a secoué [shook]
a senti [felt]
as été (tu) [were (you)]
a signifié [meant]
asperge [asparagus] (f)
assez [enough, rather]
assiette [plate] (f)
a su [knew]
a travaillé [worked]
a trouvé [found]
attendre [to wait for]
attends une minute!
    [wait a minute!]
attention! [watch out!]
attraper [to catch]
attraper un rhume [to
    catch a cold]
auberge [inn] (f)
au coin [on the corner]
aucun [any]
aujourd'hui [today]
au lieu de [instead of]
au moins [at least]
au revoir [good-bye]
aussi [too, also]
aussi . . . que [as . . . as]
automne [autumn/fall] (m)
autour [around]
au travail [at work]
autre [other]
avant [before]
avec [with]
a vécu [lived]
a vendu [sold]
avenue [avenue] (f)
avez (vous) [have (you)]
avez été (vous) [were (you)]
avion [plane] (m)
avoir [to have]
avoir à [to have to]
avoir . . . ans [to be . . . years
    old]

avoir besoin de [to need]
avoir bonne mine [to look well]
avoir chaud [to be hot]
avoir de la chance [to be lucky]
avoir envie de [to feel like]
avoir faim [to be hungry]
avoir froid [to be cold]
avoir le temps [to have (the) time]
avoir l'impression de [to feel/
   to have the feeling that]
avoir l'intention de [to plan to]
avoir mal [to hurt]
avoir peur [to be afraid]
avoir raison [to be right]
avoir soif [to be thirsty]
avoir sommeil [to be sleepy]
avoir tort [to be wrong]
a volé [flew]
a volé [stole]
avons (nous) [have (we)]
a voulu [wanted]
a voulu dire [meant]
avril [April]
a vu [saw]

b

bacon [bacon] (m)
bain [bath] (m)
balle [ball] (f)
banane [banana] (f)
bas (le) [bottom] (m)
bas [low]
base-ball [baseball] (m)
bateau [boat] (m)
beau/belle [beautiful]
beaucoup [many/much]
beaucoup de [a lot of/plenty of]
beau-père [stepfather] (m)
bébé [baby] (m)
belle-mère [stepmother] (f)
bête [stupid]
beurre [butter] (m)
bicyclette [bicycle] (f)
bien [well]
bien cuit [well-done]
bien que [although]

bien sûr [of course]
bientôt [soon]
bière [beer] (f)
bizarre [bizarre]
blague [joke] (f)
blaguer [to kid/to joke]
blanc/blanche [white]
bleu [blue]
bleu marine [navy]
boeuf [beef] (m)
boire [to drink]
boisson [drink] (f)
boîte [box] (f)
bol [bowl] (m)
bon/bonne [good]
bon après-midi [good afternoon]
bonbon [candy]
bonjour [good morning]
bon marché [cheap]
bonne [maid] (f)
bonne nuit [good night]
bonsoir [good evening]
botte [boot] (f)
bouche [mouth] (f)
boucher [butcher] (m)
boulanger [baker] (m)
bouteille [bottle] (f)
boutique [boutique] (f)
bras [arm] (m)
brun [brown]
bruit [noise] (m)

c

ça [it]
cacher [to hide]
cadeau [present/gift] (m)
café [coffee] (m)
caler [to be full]
caméra [camera] (f)
ça m'est égal [I don't care]
camion [lorry/truck] (m)
campagne [country] (f)
ça n'a aucune importance
   [never mind]
canapé [couch/sofa] (m)
canard [duck] (m)

ça ne fait rien [it doesn't matter]
ça ne marche pas [it doesn't work]
ça ne va pas [things aren't so great]
carte postale [postcard] (f)
casser [to break]
casserole [pot] (f)
ça va? [how are things?]
ce [it]
ce . . . [this]
ceci [this]
ce . . . (-là) [that]
cela [that]
cela n'a aucune importance [never mind]
cela ne fait rien [it doesn't matter]
cela ne marche pas [it won't work]
célèbre [famous]
cendrier [ashtray] (m)
cent [a hundred]
cependant [however]
cerise [cherry] (f)
ce que [what] (ce n'est pas ce que je veux = it's not what I want)
certain [certain]
certainement [certainly]
ces . . . (-ci) [these]
ces . . . (-là) [those]
cesser [to quit]
c'est ça [that's it]
ce soir [tonight]
c'est dommage [it's a pity/ a shame]
c'est l'heure [time's up]
c'est tout [that's all]
c'est vrai [that's right]
ceux . . . (-ci) [these]
ceux . . . (-là) [those]
chaise [chair] (f)
chambre [room] (f)
chambre à coucher [bedroom] (f)
changer d'avis [to change one's mind]

chanson [song] (f)
chanter [to sing]
chapeau [hat] (m)
chaque [each]
charmant [charming]
chat [cat] (m)
châtain [brown]
chaud [warm]
chaussette [sock] (f)
chaussure [shoe] (f)
chemise [shirt] (f)
chemisier [blouse] (m)
cher/chère [expensive]
chercher [to look for]
cheval [horse] (m)
cheveux [hair] (m)
chèvre [goat] (f)
chez moi [at home]
chien [dog] (m)
chocolat [chocolate] (m)
choisir [to choose]
chose [thing] (f)
chou [cabbage] (m)
chouette [swell]
cigare [cigar] (m)
cigarette [cigarette] (f)
cinéma [movies] (m)
cinq [five]
cinquante [fifty]
cinquième [fifth]
cirque [circus] (m)
citron [lemon] (m)
classe [class] (f)
clown [clown] (m)
cochon [pig] (m)
coin [corner] (m)
col roulé [polo neck/US turtleneck] (m)
combien de . . . ? [how many?]
combien de temps? [how long?]
combien est-ce? [how much is it?]
combien est-ce que ça coûte? [how much does it cost?]
comme [since]
comme [like]
comme d'habitude [as usual]

commencement [beginning/
   start] (m)
commencer [to begin/to start]
comment? [how?]
comment vous appelez-vous?
   [what's your name?]
comme vous voulez [as you like]
complet [suit] (m)
comprendre [to understand]
conduire [to drive]
confondre tout [to be mixed up]
confortable [comfortable]
connaître [to know]
connu [famous]
content [glad/pleased]
continuer [to go on/to keep
   on/to continue]
continuez! [go on!/go ahead!]
contre (être) [against (to be)]
conversation [conversation/
   talk] (f)
copain [pal] (m)
cou [neck] (m)
couleur [colour] (f)
couper [to cut]
courir [to run]
cours [class] (m)
court [short]
couteau [knife] (m)
coûter [to cost]
couverture [blanket] (f)
craie [chalk] (f)
crayon [pencil] (m)
croire [to believe]
cuiller [spoon] (f)
cuire [to cook]
cuisine [kitchen] (f)
cuisine (faire la) [cooking
   (to do)]
curieux [odd]

d
d'abord [at first]
d'accord [OK/all right]
dangereux [dangerous]
dans [in]

danse [dance] (f)
danser [to dance]
dans le coin [in the area]
de (from, of]
début [beginning/start] (m)
décembre [December]
déchirer [to tear]
décider [to decide]
définitivement [for good]
dégueulasse [lousy]
déjà [already]
déjeuner [lunch] (m)
de l' [some/any]
de la [some/any]
de la part de [on behalf of]
délicieux [delicious]
demain [tomorrow]
demander [to ask]
démarrer [to start]
demi-heure [half-hour] (f)
dent [tooth] (f)
dépêchez-vous! [hurry up!
dépendre de [to be up to
   /to depend on]
dépenser [to spend]
de quelle couleur est-ce?
   [what colour is it?]
de rien! [you're welcome!]
dernier/dernière [last]
le dernier [the last/least]
derrière [behind]
des [some/any]
déscendre [to go down]
désirer [to care for]
désolé [sorry]
dès que [as soon as]
dessert [dessert] (m)
des tas de [lots of]
de temps à autre [now and then]
de temps en temps [from
   time to time/once in a while]
détester [to hate]
de toutes façons [at any
   rate/in any case]
de toutes manières [anyway]
deux (two)

deux fois [twice]
deuxième [second]
devant [in front of]
devenir [to become]
devine! [guess!]
devoirs [homework] (m)
devoir [to have to]
devrait [should/ought to]
d'habitude [usually]
diamant [diamond] (m)
d'ici samedi [by (Saturday)]
différence [difference] (f)
différent (de) [different
    (from)]
difficile [difficult]
difficulté [difficulty] (f)
dimanche [Sunday]
dîner [dinner/supper] (m)
dingue [nuts]
dire [to tell/to say]
dire (à) [to say (to)]
disque [record] (m)
divan [couch/sofa] (m)
divorcer [to get divorced]
dix [ten]
dix-huit [eighteen]
dix-neuf [nineteen]
dix-sept [seventeen]
docteur [doctor] (m)
doigt [finger] (m)
doigt de pied [toe] (m)
doit [must/has to]
donc [so/therefore/thus]
donner [to give]
dormir [to sleep]
douche [shower] (f)
douteux [doubtful]
doux/douce [soft]
douze [twelve]
drap [sheet] (m)
drôle [funny]
du [some/any]
dur [hard]
durant [during]
durer [to last]

e
eau [water] (f)
échouer [to fail]
école [school] (f)
écouter [to listen to]
écrire [to write]
éléphant [elephant] (m)
élève [pupil] (m)
elle [she]
elles [they]
elles (obj) [them]
embrouiller tout [to be mixed up]
en [some/any]
en (dans) [in]
en avance [early]
en avoir marre [to have
    had it/to be fed up]
en avoir ras le bol [to have
    had it/to be fed up]
en bas (de l'escalier) [downstairs]
en ce moment [at present]
enchanté! [pleased to meet you!]
encore [again]
encore (toujours) [still]
encore une fois [once more]
endroit [place/spot] (m)
enfant [child] (m)
enfin [finally/at last]
en haut (de l'escalier) [upstairs]
enlever [to take off]
ennemi [enemy] (m)
ennuyeux [boring]
en pagaille [in a mess]
en retard [late]
enseigner [to teach]
ensemble [together]
ensoleillé [sunny]
ensommeillé [sleepy]
ensuite [then]
entendre [to hear]
en tout cas [in any case]
en train de [in the midst of]
entre [between]
entrer dans [to come into]
    /to enter]
entre-temps [in the mean-

time/in the meanwhile]
en vacances [on vacation]
enveloppe [envelope] (f)
environ [about/around]
envoyer [to send]
épais [thick]
épeler [to spell]
épicier [grocer] (m)
épinards [spinach] (m)
épouvantable [dreadful]
épuisé [exhausted]
erreur [error] (f)
es (tu) [are (you)]
escalier [stairs] (m)
espagnol [Spanish]
espérer [to hope]
essayer (de) [to try (to)/
    to attempt to]
essence [gas] (f)
est (il) [is (he)]
est allé [went]
est arrivé [happened/
    arrived/occurred]
est capable de [can]
est-ce qu'il vous arrive
    de . . . ? [do you ever . . . ?]
est descendu [went down]
est devenu [became]
est entré [came in]
est monté [went up]
est mort [died]
est parti [left]
est rentré [returned]
est resté [stayed]
est revenu [came back]
est sorti [went out]
est tombé [fell]
est venu [came]
et [and]
et . . . ? [what about . . . ?]
étage [floor/story] (m)
étagère [shelf] (f)
était assis [sat]
était debout [stood]
États-Unis [United States]
été [summer] (m)

éteindre [to turn off/to put off]
êtes (vous) [are you]
étrange [strange]
être [to be]
être assis [to be sitting]
être capable de [to be able to]
être censé de [to be supposed to]
être comme [to be like]
être d'accord (avec) [to
    agree (with)]
être debout [to stand/to
    be standing]
être en train de [to be (in the
    midst of) . . . + ing]
être habitué à [to be used to]
être intéressé par [to be
    interested in]
être sur le point de [to be
    about to]
étroit [narrow]
étudiant [student] (m)
étudier [to study]
eux [them]
évier [sink] (m)
exactement [exactly]
examen [test] (m)
excusez-moi [excuse me]
expliquer à [to explain to]
exprès [on purpose]
extra [great]

f

fâché contre (être) [mad]
    at, angry at (to be)]
facile [easy]
façon [way] (f)
faible [weak]
faim [hunger] (f)
faire [to do/to make]
faire attention à [to pay
    attention to]
faire des courses [to go shopping]
faire du patin à glace [to
    ice-skate]
faire du patin à roulettes
    [to roller-skate]

171

faire du ski [to go skiing]
faire la cuisine [to do the
  cooking]
faire la planche [to float]
faire la queue [to stand in line]
faire la vaisselle [to do the
  dishes]
faire mal [to hurt]
faire tomber [to drop]
faire un effort [to make an
  effort]
faire un voyage [to make a trip]
fais attention! [be careful!]
fait [does]
falloir [to have to]
famille [family] (f)
fatigué [tired]
faute [mistake] (f)
faux/fausse [false/fake]
favori/favorite [favourite]
femme [woman] (f)
femme [wife] (f)
femme de chambre [maid] (f)
fenêtre [window] (f)
ferme [farm] (f)
fermé [closed]
fermer [to close/to shut]
fermier [farmer] (m)
feu [fire] (m)
février [February]
fille [girl] (f)
fille [daughter] (f)
film [film/movie] (m)
fils [son] (m)
fin [end] (f)
finir [to finish]
fleur [flower] (f)
flic [cop] (m)
fois (une) [once]
football [Association football]
football américain [football] (m)
forêt [forest] (f)
fort [strong]
fou [crazy]
foulard [scarf] (m)
fourchette [fork] (f)

fraise [strawberry] (f)
français [French]
France [France]
fréquemment [frequently]
frère [brother] (m)
fric ['bread'] (m)
frites [French fries] (f)
froid [cold]
fromage [cheese] (m)
fruit [fruit] (m)
fumer [to smoke]

g
gagner [to win]
gants [gloves] (m)
garçon [boy, waiter] (m)
garder [to keep]
gare [train station] (f)
gâteau [cake] (m)
gauche (à) [left (on the)]
gendarme [policeman] (m)
généralement [generally]
genre [kind] (m)
gens [people] (m)
gentil/gentille [kind/nice]
glace [ice cream] (f)
gosse [kid] (m)
grand [big]
grand [tall]
grand magasin [department
  store] (m)
grand-mère [grandmother] (f)
grand-père [grandfather] (m)
grands-parents [grandparents] (m)
grave [serious]
grimper [to climb]
gris [grey]
gros/grosse [fat]
grossier [rude]

h
habiter (à) [to live (in)]
haïr [to hate]
haricots verts [string beans] (m)
haut [top] (m)
haut [high]

herbe [grass] (f)
heure [hour] (f)
(5) heures [(5) o'clock]
heureusement [happily]
heureux/heureuse [happy]
hier [yesterday]
hier soir [last night]
histoire [story] (f)
hiver [winter] (m)
hobby [hobby] (m)
homme [man] (m)
horrible [horrible]
hôtel [hotel] (m)
huit [eight]

i
ici [here]
il [he]
ils [they]
il est (5) heures (10) [it's (10) past (5)]
il est (dix) heures et demie [it's half past (ten)]
il est (5) heures moins (10) [it's (10) to (5)]
il est (dix) heures moins le quart [it's a quarter to (ten)]
il est (dix) heures trente [it's (ten) thirty]
il fait beau [it's nice out]
il faut (partir) [you have to/ must (leave)]
il neige [it's snowing]
il n'y a pas longtemps [not long ago]
il pleut [it's raining]
il y a [there is/there are]
il y a (5 ans) [(five years) ago]
immédiatement [immediately]
imperméable [raincoat] (m)
important [important]
incendie [fire] (m)
inconfortable [uncomfortable]
inconnu [unknown]
infirmière [nurse] (f)

injuste [unfair]
intelligent [clever/intelligent]
intentionnellement [intentionally]
interdire [to forbid]
intéressant [interesting]
inviter [to invite]
invraisemblable (c'est) [unlikely (it's)]
Italie [Italy] (f)
italien [Italian]

j
j'aimerais mieux [I'd rather]
jamais [never]
jambe [leg] (f)
jambon [ham] (m)
janvier [January]
jardin [garden] (m)
jardinier [gardener] (m)
jaune [yellow]
je [I]
jeans [jeans] (m)
je crois bien [I believe so/I guess so]
je pense que oui [I think so/I suppose to]
je préfère [I prefer/I'd rather]
j'espère bien [I hope so]
je suppose [I guess so]
jeter [to throw]
jeu [game] (m)
jeudi [Thursday]
jeune [young]
joli [pretty]
jouer [to play]
jouer un tour à [to play a trick on]
jouet [toy] (m)
jour [day] (m)
jour férié [holiday] (m)
journal [newspaper] (m)
juillet [July]
juin [June]
jupe [skirt] (f)
jusqu'à [until]

juste [just]
juste [fair]
juste au cas où [just in case]

l

la (art) [the]
la (obj) [it/her]
là [there]
la fermer [to shut up]
laid [ugly]
laisser [to let]
laisser tomber [to drop]
laisser qqn tranquille
    [to leave s.o. alone]
lait [milk] (m)
laitue [lettuce] (f)
lampe [lamp] (f)
la plupart de [most]
large [wide/broad]
le (art) [the]
le (obj) [it/him]
leçon [lesson] (f)
léger [light]
légume [vegetable] (m)
lent [slow]
lentement [slowly]
lentilles de contact
    [contact lenses] (f)
lequel? [which?]
les (art) [the]
les (obj) [them]
les deux [both]
lettre [letter] (f)
leur (adj) [their]
leur (obj) [them]
leur (le) [theirs]
libre [free]
linge [laundry] (m)
lion [lion] (m)
lire [to read]
lit [bed] (m)
livre [book] (m)
loin [far]
Londres [London]
long/longue [long]
lourd [heavy]

lui [it/her/him]
lundi [Monday]
lunettes [glasses] (f)

m

ma [my]
magasin [store/shop] (m)
magazine [magazine] (m)
mai [May]
main [hand] (f)
maintenant [now]
mais [but]
maison [house/home] (f)
malade [ill/sick]
mal de gorge [sore throat] (m)
mal de tête [headache] (m)
malgré [in spite of]
malheureusement [unhappily]
malheureux/malheureuse
    [unhappy]
malin [clever]
mal rangé [sloppy]
manger [to eat]
manière [way] (f)
manteau [coat] (m)
marcher [to walk]
mardi [Tuesday]
mari [husband] (m)
marron [brown]
mars [March]
matin [morning] (m)
mauvais [bad]
me [me]
mec [guy] (m)
méchant [mean, nasty]
médecin [doctor] (m)
meilleur [better]
meilleur (le) [best (the)]
même [even]
même (le) [same (the)]
menu [menu] (m)
merci [thank you]
mercredi [Wednesday]
mère [mother] (f)
merveilleux [wonderful/
    marvellous]

mes [my]
Métro [subway/underground] (m)
mettre [to put]
mettre [to put on]
meubles [furniture] (m)
midi (à) [noon (at)]
mien (le) [mine]
mieux [better]
mieux (le) [best (the)]
mille [a thousand]
mince [thin]
minuit (à) [midnight (at)]
minute [minute] (f)
moche [crummy]
moi [me]
moi aussi [me too]
moins [less]
mois [month] (m)
moment [moment] (m)
mon [my]
montagne [mountain] (f)
monter [to go up]
montre [watch] (f)
montrer [to show]
monument [monument] (m)
moquette [carpet] (f)
morceau [piece] (m)
mou [soft]
mouchoir [handkerchief] (m)
mouillé [wet]
mourir [to die]
mourir de faim [to be
    starving/to be starved]
mur [wall] (m)
musée [museum] (m)
musique [music] (f)

n
nager [to swim]
naître [to be born]
nana [broad] (f)
n'a pas fait [didn't do]
ne fait pas [doesn't do]
neige [snow] (f)
neiger [to snow]
ne . . . jamais [never/ever]

n'en a pas [not to have any]
ne pas [not/doesn't/hasn't]
ne pas être d'accord [to disagree]
ne pas prêter attention
    à qqn [to ignore s.o.]
ne peut pas [can't]
n'est pas capable de [can't]
ne plus [not any longer/
    not any more]
ne plus avoir faim [to be full]
neuf [nine]
neuf/neuve [new]
neveu [nephew] (m)
New-York [New York]
nez [nose] (m)
nièce [niece] (f)
Noël [Christmas]
noir [black]
nom [name] (m)
non [no]
non plus [not either]
nos [our]
note [bill/check] (f)
notre [our]
nôtre (le) [ours]
nourriture [food] (f)
nous [we]
nous (obj) [us]
nouveau/nouvelle [new]
novembre [November]
nuit [night] (f)
nulle part [nowhere/not
    anywhere]

o
obtenir [to get/to obtain]
occupé [busy]
octobre [October]
œil [eye] (m)
œuf [egg] (m)
oiseau [bird] (m)
OK [OK]
oncle [uncle] (m)
ont (ils) [have (they)]
ont été (ils) [were (they)]
onze [eleven]

orange [orange] (f)
oreille [ear] (f)
oreiller [pillow] (m)
ou [or]
où [where]
oublier [to forget]
oui [yes]
ours [bear] (m)
ouvert [open]
ouvrir [to open]

p
pagaille [mess] (f)
page [page] (f)
pain [bread] (m)
pamplemousse [grapefruit] (m)
pantalon [slacks/trousers] (m)
pantoufles [slippers] (f)
papier [paper] (m)
Pâques [Easter]
par (avion) [by (plane)]
parapluie [umbrella] (m)
par bonheur [luckily]
parc [park] (m)
parce que [because]
parent [relative] (m)
parents [parents] (m)
paresseux [lazy]
par exemple [for example/
    for instance]
parfois [sometimes]
parfum [flavour] (m)
par hasard [by chance]
parier [to bet]
Paris [Paris]
parler avec/à [to talk to/
    with, to speak to/with]
par malheur [unluckily]
par terre [on the floor]
partir [to leave]
partout [everywhere/all over]
pas assez [not . . . enough]
pas encore [not yet]
passer (un examen) [to
    take (a test)]
passe-temps [pastime] (m)

passionnant [exciting]
pas si . . . que [not as . . . as]
patin [skate] (m)
patiner [to skate]
pauvre [poor]
payer [to pay]
pays [country] (m)
peintre [painter] (m)
pellicule [photographic film] (f)
pendant (l'été) [during (the
    summer)]
pendant (dix ans) [for (ten
    years)]
pendant que [while]
penser [to think]
perdre [to lose]
père [father] (m)
personne [no one]
personne [person] (f)
personnes (des) [people]
petit [small/short]
petit coin (le) [john (the)] (m)
petit-déjeuner [breakfast] (m)
petit-enfant [grandchild] (m)
petite-fille [granddaughter] (f)
petit-fils [grandson] (m)
petits-pois [peas] (m)
peu [little/a few]
peu profond [shallow]
peut [can]
peut-être [maybe/perhaps]
photographie [photo] (f)
pièce [room] (f)
pied [foot] (m)
pilote [pilot] (m)
pipe [pipe] (f)
pire [worse]
pire (le) [worst (the)]
piscine [pool] (f)
placard [closet, cupboard] (m)
plafond [ceiling] (m)
plage [beach] (f)
plaisanter [to kid/to joke]
plaisanterie [joke] (f)
planche à voile [windsurfer] (f)
plante [plant] (f)

plein [full]
pleurer [to cry]
pleuvoir [to rain]
pluie [rain] (f)
plus [more, -er]
plus (le) [most (the)]
plus ou moins [more or less]
plus . . . que [more . . . than]
plusieurs [several]
plus tard [later]
plus tôt [earlier]
plutôt [pretty]
poche [pocket] (f)
poêle [pan] (f)
poire [pear] (f)
poisson [fish] (m)
poivre [pepper] (m)
poli [polite]
pomme [apple] (f)
pomme de terre [potato] (f)
pompier [fireman] (m)
porte [door] (f)
portefeuille [wallet] (m)
porter [to carry]
porter [to wear]
poser une question [to ask a
    question]
poulet [chicken] (m)
pour [for]
pour + verbe [to/in order to]
pourboire [tip] (m)
pour que [so that]
pourquoi? [why?]
pourvu que [provided that]
pousser [to push]
pouvoir [to be able to]
préféré [favourite]
préférer [to prefer]
premier/première [first]
prendre [to take]
prendre rendez-vous [to
    make an appointment]
prendre son temps [to take
    one's time]
prendre un bain [to take a bath]
près [near]

pressé [in a hurry]
prêt [ready]
prêter [to lend]
printemps [spring] (m)
prix [price] (m)
probablement [probably]
problème [problem] (m)
prochain [next]
professeur [teacher] (m)
profond [deep]
propre [clean]
puis [then]
puisque [since]
pull [sweater] (m)
pull-over [pullover] (m)
purée [mashed potatoes] (f)

q
quand [when]
quarante [forty]
quart d'heure [quarter of
    an hour] (m)
quatorze [fourteen]
quatre [four]
quatre-vingt [eighty]
quatre-vingt-dix [ninety]
quatrième [fourth]
que . . . [than . . .]
que (conj) [that]
que (rel) [that/which/ who(m)]
que? [what?]
quel? [which/what?]
quel âge avez vous? [how old
    are you?]
quelle heure est-il? [what
    time is it?]
quelle histoire! [what a fuss!]
quelque chose [anything/
    something]
quelquefois [sometimes]
quelque part [somewhere/
    anywhere]
quelques [some/a few]
quelqu'un [someone/anyone]
qu'est-ce que c'est? [what is it?]
qu'est-ce qu'il y a? [what's up?]

qu'est-ce qui ne va pas?
  [what's wrong?]
question [question] (f)
queue [tail] (f)
qui [that]
qui [who]
qui [which]
qui a sommeil [sleepy]
qui est en train de [in the
  midst of (doing)]
quinze [fifteen]
quoi [what]
quoi de neuf? [what's new?]
quoique [although]

r
raconter [to tell]
radio [radio] (f)
ramasser [to pick up]
rangé [tidy]
rapide [quick/fast]
rapidement [quickly/rapidly]
rarement [rarely/seldom]
récemment [recently]
recevoir [to get/to receive]
regarder [to look at]
règle [ruler] (f)
rencontrer [to meet]
rendez-vous [appointment] (m)
rendre service [to do a favour]
repas [meal] (m)
répéter [to repeat]
répondre [to answer]
réponse [answer] (f)
ressembler [to be like/
  to resemble]
restaurant [restaurant] (m)
rester [to stay/to remain]
restez tranquille! [stay still!]
retourner [to return]
réussir [to succeed]
rêve [dream] (m)
réveil [clock] (m)
revenir [to come back]
rêver [to dream]
rhume [cold] (m)

riche [rich]
rire [to laugh]
rideau [curtain] (m)
rien [nothing]
robe [dress] (f)
roman [novel] (m)
rouge [red]
route [road] (f)
rubis [ruby] (m)
rue [street] (f)

s
sa [her/his/its]
sable [sand] (m)
sac [bag] (m)
sac à main [handbag, (US)
  purse] (m)
sage [good, well-behaved]
s'agir de [to be about]
saignant [rare]
sait [can]
salade [salad] (f)
sale [dirty]
salle à manger [dining room] (f)
salle de bain [bathroom] (f)
salle de séjour [living room] (f)
salon [living room] (m)
salut! [hi!]
salut! [bye!]
samedi [Saturday]
s'amuser bien [to have a
  good time]
sans [without]
s'asseoir [to sit (down)]
sauf [except]
savoir [to know]
savoir (faire) [to know (how to)]
savon [soap] (m)
se battre [to fight]
sec [dry]
seconde [second] (f)
secouer [to shake]
se décider [to make up
  one's mind]
se demander si [to wonder if]
se dépêcher [to rush/to hurry]

se déshabiller [to get undressed]
seize [sixteen]
sel [salt] (m)
se laver [to get washed]
se lever [to get up]
se lever [to stand up]
semaine [week] (f)
semblable à [similar to]
s'en aller [to go away]
s'endormir [to fall asleep]
se marier [to get married]
se moquer de [to laugh at]
se noyer [to drown]
sens [meaning] (m)
sentir [to feel]
se passer [to happen]
se presser [to rush]
se produire [to occur]
sept [seven]
septembre [September]
se reposer [to rest]
se réveiller [to wake up]
sérieux [serious]
serpent [snake] (m)
serveur [waiter] (m)
serveuse [waitress] (f)
serviette [towel] (f)
serviette de table [napkin] (f)
ses [her/his/its]
se souvenir de [to remember]
s'est battu [fought]
seul [alone]
seulement [only]
s'habiller [to get dressed]
si [if]
si (gentil) [so (kind)]
sien (le) [hers/its/his]
signifier [to mean]
s'il vous plaît [please]
simple [simple]
simplement [simply]
singe [monkey] (m)
six [six]
skier [to ski]
sœur [sister] (f)
soir [evening] (m)

soixante [sixty]
soixante-dix [seventy]
soleil [sun] (m)
sommes (nous) [are (we)]
son [her/his/its]
sont (ils) [are (they)]
sorte [sort] (f)
sortir [to go out]
soudain [suddenly, all of
   a sudden]
souhaiter [to wish]
soupe [soup] (f)
souris [mouse] (m)
sous [under]
souvent [often]
spaghetti [spaghetti] (m)
sport [sports] (m)
station-service [service/gas
   station] (f)
steak [steak] (m)
stupide [stupid]
stylo [pen] (m)
sucre [sugar] (m)
sucré [sweet]
suis (je) [am (I)]
suivant [following/next]
supposer [to suppose]
sur [on]
sûr [safe, sure]
surtout [especially/above all]
sympa [nice]

t
ta [your]
table [table] (f)
tableau noir [blackboard] (m)
taille [size] (f)
tailleur [suit] (m)
tandis que [while]
tant mieux [all the better]
tante [aunt] (f)
tant pis [too bad]
tapis [rug] (m)
tard [late]
tasse [cup] (f)
te [you]

télé [TV] (f)
téléphone [telephone] (m)
téléphoner [to phone/to
   call up/to ring up]
télévision [television] (f)
tellement [so]
tennis [tennis] (m)
tenter [to attempt]
terre [land] (f)
terrible [dreadful]
tes [your]
tête [head] (f)
thé [tea] (m)
tien (le) [yours]
tigre [tiger] (m)
timbre [stamp] (m)
tirer [to pull]
toi [you]
toilettes [toilet/bathroom] (f)
tomate [tomato] (f)
tomber [to fall]
ton [your]
tôt [early]
toujours [always]
toujours (encore) [still]
tour [turn] (m)
tous [all]
tous les deux [both]
tous les (jours) [every (day)]
tous les combien? [how often?]
tout [everything]
tout à coup [all of a sudden]
tout à fait [quite]
tout de suite [right away/
   right now/at once]
tout le monde [everyone]
train [train] (m)
travail [work] (m)
travailler [to work]
treize [thirteen]
trente [thirty]
très [very]
très bien [fine]
très chaud [hot]
triste [sad]
trois [three]

troisième [third]
trop [too/too many/much]
trouver [to find]
truc [thing] (m)
tu [you]
type [fellow] (m)

u
un/une [an, a]
un [one]
un autre [another]
une fois [once]
un peu [a bit/a little]

v
vacances [vacation] (f)
vache [cow] (f)
vallée [valley] (f)
vanille [vanilla] (f)
veau [veal] (m)
vélo [bike] (m)
vendre [to sell]
vendredi [Friday]
venir [to come]
venir de [to (have) just]
verre [glass] (m)
vert [green]
veste [jacket] (f)
vêtements [clothes] (m)
viande [meat] (f)
vide [empty]
vieux, vieille [old]
vilain [nasty/naughty]
vin [wine] (m)
vingt [twenty]
violon d'Ingres [hobby/
   pastime] (m)
visage [face] (m)
vite [quickly/fast]
vivre (à) [to live (in)]
voir [to see]
voisin [neighbour] (m)
voiture [car] (f)
voler [to steal]
voler [to fly]
volley-ball [volleyball] (m)

vous (obj) [yours]
votre [your]
vôtre (le) [yours]
vouloir [to want]
vouloir dire [to mean]
vous [you]
vous (obj.) [yours]
vous comprenez? [do you
    understand?]
vous trouvez? [do you think so?]
voyage [trip] (m)

voyager [to travel]
vrai [true/real]
vraiment [really]
vraisemblable (c'est)
    [likely (it's]

y
yeux [eyes] (m)

z
zoo [zoo] (m)